CLIMATE CYCLE

CLIMATE CYCLE

Why a ride around Britain became a movement for change

KATE STRONG

© 2024 Kate Strong

All rights reserved.

ISBN: 9798325841767

No part of this publication may be reproduced, distributed, or transmitted in any form or by any means, including photocopying, recording, or other electronic or mechanical methods, without the prior written permission of the publisher, except in the case of brief quotations embodied in critical reviews and certain other non-commercial uses permitted by copyright law.

Every reasonable effort has been made to contact copyright holders of material. Reproduced in this book. If any have inadvertently been overlooked, the author and publisher (same person) would be glad to hear from them and make good in future editions any errors or omissions brought to their attention.

This book is loosely linked to real life events, locales, and persons. The views and opinions expressed in this book are my own and do not necessarily reflect those of any organisation or other individuals.

*Change is inevitable.
We can wait and react to it,
or step up and create a new path and a new world.*

Praise

Kate Strong is a warrior woman and beautiful human. This is a wonderful book about her journey to exercise her way out of heartbreak and then use her amazing athletic achievements to tackle the climate emergency and make a better world for us all. It will motivate you to jump on your bike and go on your own adventure, and never eat farmed salmon again in your life! Read it and be inspired!

Jessica Hepburn, author & adventure activist. First woman to complete the Sea Street Summit Challenge - summit Mount Everest, swim the English Channel & run the London marathon

To say Kate's achievements have been phenomenal is an understatement. To use her skills and achievements for a higher purpose is truly inspiring. This book is a call to action. Our planet and humanity are in trouble, yet we have the ability to heal. This beautifully written book is a must read for us all and shows that no action is too small. We can all play our part to be the change we want to witness in this world we share.

Dr Shireen Kassam, Doctor and Director of Plant-Based Health Professionals UK

A valuable opportunity to see the experiences that sit behind Kate's astounding World Records and Climate Cycle, and to the formidable woman she is. In this book Kate triumphs in bringing the same passion to her writing as she's brought to each of her previous feats.

Melissa Wilson, former GB Rower and co-founder of climate non-profit Athletes of the World

This book is a page-turner. It immediately draws you in with some incredible and hilarious stories, told beautifully from Kate's refreshing view of the world.
As Kate tells her story that takes her to her arduous and physically painful climate cycle, she exposes us to thought-provoking views on how to shift your own perspective - how this shift often accompanies big sporting challenges. She provides an inspiring and refreshing view on the human need to connect to other communities and people.
Honest and heartfelt, the books helps us to make sense of our feelings about the diminishing world around us whilst also appreciating the beauty of this world and humanity as it is now.
Katie Cross, founder & CEO of Pledgeball

What a ride and what an inspiration. Sport and the world urgently need more Kate Strongs!
Damian Hall, ultrarunner, author, activist

In Climate Cycle, the aptly named adventurer Kate Strong takes the reader on her this-should-be-a-movie journey of building strength by taking on absurdly difficult challenges, falling down, getting back up, learning from mistakes, and coming out ever, well, stronger. As she tells the tale of her 3,000+ mile, 3-month climate cycle around the mainland Britain, we can feel her struggles, cope with her fits and starts, and rally behind her as she keeps pedalling. How Strong applies these lessons to an even bigger test — the climate fight — is the true worth of this must read volume.
Lew Blaustein, Founder EcoAthletes & Green Sports Blog

Immensely inspirational and grippingly honest. This is a timely reminder of the impact just one person can make and how we can all lean on each other for encouragement, support, and inspiration in our own journeys to becoming a climate champion!
David Wheeler, Professional footballer & climate advocate

This story of an extraordinary endeavour and the life journey which led to it is revealed in a beautiful, empowering and brave style by someone I could only describe as 'epic'! Joining the dots between a wonderfully interesting collection of examples of Earth-protecting action from her Climate Cycle, Kate's adventures contain lessons which we can all learn from and be inspired by.
Etienne Stott, Olympic gold medallist London 2012

From hard facts to home truths, Kate takes us not only on a climate cycle but on a journey of a lifetime. The strength and vulnerability shown by Kate to explore the depths of her being alongside the intricate connections and reality of her homeland will fill anyone reading with inspiration, awe and the courage to change!
Katie Rood, Athlete Activist, Former player for Juventus, Lewes FC, Southampton FC and the New Zealand National Team

Kate Strong's Climate Cycle is a powerful narrative highlighting community, collaboration, and compassion. Kate's journey inspires proactive climate action, showcasing the importance of creating positive change rather than reacting to environmental degradation. Her life's dedication moves the dial toward a sustainable future, inspiring others to join the movement for a better world. We need more leaders like Kate.
Isaac Kenyon, Eco Adventurer, Environmental Sustainability & Wellbeing Advocate and Endurance Record Holder

Brilliantly written, gripping and inspiring story of Kate Strong's life which is filled with incredible challenges and achievements. The learnings collected from communities visited on her recent Climate Cycle are valuable for us all.
Laura Baldwin, Olympic sailor, coach and environmental activist

Join Kate on her transformative journey of self-discovery, as she trades convention for adventure. After completing her formal education, she ditched the 'good girl' script and embarked on a global odyssey. But 'settling down' only led to disillusionment. Some souls are meant to soar, and Kate's is one of them. She cycled across the island on a bamboo frame bike for 90 days, immersing herself in nature and igniting a passion for environmental stewardship. Now, she shares her insights on how small changes can make a big impact on the climate - and she's just getting started!
Pragnya Mohan, India's top triathlete, TEDx Speaker, Founder of Ek Beti Ek Cycle (One Daughter One Cycle)

In this delightful, moving and inspiring little book, Kate Strong, does something that few people have the integrity and courage to do; commit to leading a life principled on protecting the environment against the ever-present spectre of climate change. This book is a reminder that all of us, no matter the size or stature of our platforms or resources have the moral and ethical duty to stand up for what is right and good for our planet. We all share planet earth, and we must learn to live in relative harmony, with all living things, great and small, if we are to inherit a world that is amendable to human civilisation as we know it. In this book, Kate Strong attempts to show us how!
Dr Numair Masud, Freshwater Scientist, Cardiff University

An inspiring personal adventure of boldly stepping into your unknown on what you can do to act on climate change.
David Gent, CEO, Active Humber

Table of contents

Foreword by Dave Cornthwaite 12
Introduction 16
The good girl 18
Drifting with the clouds 36
Being selfish is the most selfless thing you can do 64
You're at the top, so what? 79
Why now? 88
More than a bike ride 92
What is sustainability? 96
High expectations set you up for high disappointment 107
Be in the question 116
The thread connecting the projects 119
The air we breathe 125
Girls (even climate-aware ones) just want to have fun 127
Keep the goal in stone and the journey in sand 138
The heavens have opened 148
Home is where I lay my head 154
Hypocrite 163
Does recycling actually work? 169
The world is what we eat 174
Lower the cost 182
Only dead fish flow with the current 184
Community spirit 189
I had more punctures than flies in my mouth 194
Is there hope? 200
With gratitude 206
Resources 211
About the author 214

Foreword by Dave Cornthwaite

When, after years of self propelled journeys on all manners of wonderfully slow transport somehow delivered me into a more settled existence as the co-creator of a camping farm in Lincolnshire, I always hoped that now and then other folks on their own non motorised adventures would stop by. 'If you build it, they will come' is just as appropriate a motto as the endlessly optimistic 'Say Yes More!' that had guided my often unskilled choices for a couple of decades. And after a while folks did indeed start to walk and bike up our track in the hopes of finding a fluffy piece of grass to camp on, if not a slightly more comfortable glampy option in a bus, pod, hut or hammock.

Some adventurers just ride in and others get in touch in advance, and it's the latter who tend to have a plan greater than just some freedom and time on the road. Kate contacted me a solid six months before we met in June 2023, just a few days into her journey, and incredibly she was just one day off her original estimate.

I always see it as a test when someone visits the Big Sky Hideaway on a bicycle, panniers laden and skin weathered. Do their eyes shine? Are they on a mission? Is there any feeling about what they're experiencing or is this just something to do? And heck, does seeing them on the move make me finally want to get out there and test out my body and mind again? So far, each visit has just reminded me that for now I'm in the right place, doing the right thing, staying there and travelling 10km a day in circles with a drill in one hand and alpaca feed in the other. But boy do I love meeting people who are properly living.

Kate is one of those humans. This lady has spirit by the gallon and an admirable cause to boot. I tried to remind her not to forget about the beautiful simplicity of just... riding, because she was so focused on talking about her Climate Cycle - the mission, not the journey. Of course, there's room for both, and after a night in our YesBus (which we often offer a night or two in to brilliant people doing brilliant things) Kate welcomed in the local BBC crew to discuss cycling, the climate and adventure.

In an era marked by profound environmental challenges and an urgent call for sustainable action, we need to be more like Kate. 'Climate Cycle' emerges as a beacon of hope and a roadmap for transformative change. Kate, a renowned environmental advocate and adventurer, has dedicated her life to championing the cause of our planet. Her unique perspective, forged through personal experience and relentless advocacy, is both inspiring and essential.

'Climate Cycle' is more than a book; it is a testament to the power of individual and collective action in the face of climate adversity. Kate's journey is a compelling narrative that intertwines her passion for cycling with her unwavering commitment to environmental stewardship. Her story is not only about miles covered and terrains conquered but also about the communities she has touched and the awareness she raised along the way.

Throughout this book, readers will be captivated by Kate's vivid storytelling, her encounters with diverse cultures, and her unyielding resolve to make a difference. Her insights into the interconnectedness of global ecosystems and human resilience offer valuable lessons for anyone seeking to understand and combat climate change. Kate's narrative is a clarion call to all of us to recognise our role in this global effort and to take meaningful steps towards a sustainable future.

As you embark on this journey through the pages of 'Climate Cycle' prepare to be inspired by Kate Strong's indomitable spirit and her unwavering belief in the possibility of change. This book is a rallying cry for action, a celebration of human potential, and a testament to the enduring power of hope.

Introduction

I used to say that my background, and who I am, is largely unimportant to the narrative of what I've accomplished, but isn't entirely true, because, even though I believe that many people have the capacity to do what I do, not many people actually start, let alone fail and continue onwards until, on a couple of occasions, the goal is achieved. The experiences I have lived through are the foundations upon which I build and fuel my desire to keep evolving. My past has forged my personality, carved my values and designed the canvas I paint my actions upon today. For this reason, even though the inspiration for writing this book was to share the discoveries made through my British cycle, I feel it important to also share a bit about who I am. Just like in nature, we cannot segregate each species and expect the flowers to flourish without the soil or insects interacting with it, I too cannot be separated from the Climate Cycle. Our paths are eternally linked and to pull us apart would leave either story feeling unbalanced somehow.

At 44 years' old, it would have been fair to assume that I was clear in who I was and why I was attempting such an extreme cycle. Yet, in honesty, I was struggling and needed a big distraction from the more personal, and potentially more confronting, concerns I had about the direction of my life. Having just gone through yet another breakup and with concerns about my financial instability, as well as how - if at all - I could make a dent in the ever growing subject of sustainability and climate crisis, a 3-month cycle around Britain seemed ridiculous at best.

Yet, I've learned over the years that whenever my attention spirals downwards into ever growing circles of self-flagellation and overwhelm, movement can distract my typical negative thought patterns. The larger the downward circles, the larger the movement needs to be. And so, the adventure called Climate Cycle was born.

The Climate Cycle could be perceived as a 'success' because I achieved what I set out to do: I cycled over 3,000 miles (7,770 km) on a hand-made bamboo bike around Britain. From one angle, it was a success because I finished where I started, as per the plan. Yet, success is subjective and very limited in scope, not allowing the subtle ripples of life to ebb and flow between feeling as if we're flying towards, or falling away from whatever we embarked upon.

In this book, my intention is to share what was going on underneath the perceived calm water I was gliding over, because I can assure you, throughout the 90 days, I was anything but calm!

This book does talk about the fifty communities and projects I visited, the people who generously offered me a spare room to sleep in as well as the route I cycled. Yet, if you are expecting a typical adventure book, you will be disappointed. The Climate Cycle became as much a personal exploration seeking hope, resilience and growth as discovering the activities British-based individuals are taking to address the climate crisis.

The good girl

As Steve Jobs famously said, 'you can't connect the dots looking forward; you can only connect them looking backward.' Hopefully, you'll start to see the dots connecting and designing the path that led me to who I am today.

I've always felt like an outsider, or a better description is an observer to my own life. I rarely felt like I fully fitted-in, I struggled to believe that I lived up to what was expected of me, but I also have a naturally rebellious streak to defiantly forge my own path, though this latter aspect of my personality took a few decades to find its voice.

Born to a typically traditional Welsh family, I grew up in a household where my father worked hard at building his own company to provide for his wife and children. Meanwhile, my mother stayed at home, caring for and supporting my younger brother and me in our numerous hobbies. We were transported to athletic clubs, cross country running training, rugby matches, and swimming galas. Rarely were we met with a 'no,' and almost every evening and weekend were filled with activities and adventure.

As a fiercely independent girl growing up in such a traditional household, where my father was unquestionably the authority figure, I learnt early on that I needed to comply and become the model daughter that was expected of me. On the few rare occasions I stepped out of line, typically saying something that was too harsh or close to the truth, rather than intentional malice, I was reprimanded, and the belief that I needed to be a 'good girl' was reinforced.

I did well at school, and it was obvious to all but me that I'd attend university. Within the UK, the year I graduated from school would be the last year where university education was offered for free, and the assurance of not accruing debt while studying, as well as the prestige it would bring my family because I would be the first person to attend university, was too great an opportunity to miss. Reasoning with my parents that, at seventeen, I had no idea what I wanted for breakfast most mornings, let alone my future career path, fell on deaf ears. I wanted to travel the world and explore the sticky, humid rainforests of Amazonia and live in hand-made huts hugging the side of a mountain, sharing a steamy broth served in a wooden bowl with native tribal communities who spoke a foreign and distant language. I wanted to run my fingers across the uneven walls of ancient and almost forgotten civilisations and experience them being brought to life by the shadows of a crackling fire dancing with whispers of the stories shared between the soil and the animals. I wanted, exhausted from climbing, to scream from the peak of a mountain and have no one hear me but for the distant replies from exotic birds. I wanted to only own what I could carry on my back, to sleep wherever and whenever I felt tired, and my evening lullabies to be the sounds of the lapping ocean on a sandy beach.

I wanted to discover the world and who I am. And I desperately wanted to break free from the constraints and rules I had been conforming to for all my life and feel the rawness of being alive!

Yet, back then, I didn't know how to explain any of this, and my feeble response, 'I don't know what I want to do,' offered as a counter to why I shouldn't go to university wasn't enough to change the path already chosen for me.

One concession was made, and instead of a purely practical and mathematical-based course, I was allowed to apply for, and was later accepted to study, Environmental Engineering. The environmental element of the course was a nod to the natural world I craved. I had found a small crack to slide my desire for wilderness into what was set to be five years of otherwise structured and uncreative study.

One aspect of my personality is once I start something - by desire or through enforcement - I surrender to the task at hand. Realising that I would be spending half a decade studying engineering, I fully immersed myself into the subject. Even though I found most of the topics dull and uninteresting, I started to see opportunities to leverage my fate and introduce travel, albeit under the guise as an engineering student. One summer I was accepted to work as a research student at the University of Moscow, which funded my trip to study Spanish in Cuba later that same year. I was also accepted to complete a Masters in engineering from a French university, enabling me to live in France as a resident for two years. Still hungry for more experience and travel, I found a work placement in the romantic city of Florence, Italy for my final six months of my Masters degree. Not being able to speak a word of Italian excited me more than concerned me. I craved immersing myself in a culture that was foreign to me.

Even though I had found a way to enjoy my degree - through travelling and studying abroad - I was still counting down the days until I graduated and was free to truly explore. That day finally arrived and I graduated with a first class with honours Bachelor degree and two Masters degrees. I had played the 'good daughter' role to the best of my ability, my parents had the family graduation photo to share with their friends, and I could finally pack my bag and fulfil what I had been dreaming of since I was a young girl.

As a congratulatory gift for graduating, my parents had bought me a 'round the world trip' comprising six one-way flights to any destinations of my choice. Gripping tightly to this ticket, I boarded a flight destined for Mexico City and the first day of complete freedom. Within 24 hours of arriving, I realised that I needed to remove my rose-tinted glasses from travelling and had to start being a bit more responsible about looking after myself. Being 5'9" (175 cm) with long blond hair and blue eyes, I would never look like a Mexican local, whose skin and hair colour conjured up different tones of coffee, and most people struggled to reach my shoulders in height. Yet, wearing pigtails and a powder-pink top only highlighted the naivety of my foreignness and, unbeknown to me, it was bound to attract unwanted attention.

My first day in the largest city I had ever been to in my life - Mexico DF - I was early to meet a friend's sister who agreed to show me around the National Museum. Innocently enough, I decided to explore a local park instead of sitting in the museum cafe and, with wide eyes, I followed the path deeper and deeper into the park. The path originally started meandering through carefully manicured gardens designed on European Renaissance patterns. Hungry to see something more authentic, I turned off the main path and started following a smaller route where the surrounding foliage slowly grew from shrubs to hedges and trees enclosing me tightly to the path. It wasn't long until the path had narrowed again, and what started out as manicured gardens - sprouting exotic and brightly coloured flowers emitting an elixir of scents - closed in on me, squeezing out the coloured flowers and replacing it with tall, dense green walls of foliage.

My smile and wonder transitioned to a frown and an acute awareness that I wasn't alone. Unconsciously pulling my rucksack closer to me, I turned around, hoping I could find my way back to where I started. But just as I turned I saw a man emerge from the bushes in front of me. Now realising that the path I had been following ended by a busy road, I had nowhere to run. Plus, glancing down, I saw that he was wielding a knife.

'Give me your things,' he said in Spanish, voice shaking.

Looking down into his eyes (because even robbers, it appeared, were much shorter than me), I could only see fear just before he pulled his glance away nervously. I paused. Having lived as an observer for most of my life, I was able to see the scene between me, a young and ignorant traveller, and this man, a frightened local, from a point of objectivity. I didn't feel afraid or at risk, so I just stood there, looking at him.

The long pause was finally broken by the man. 'Can't you see I have a knife? Give me your things,' he said, waggling what was quite a small knife, with a blade no longer than 4 cm (1.5 inches), at a guess.

I smiled and gently said, 'no'.

Either my response or how I delivered it stunned this guy into confusion. 'Why not?' he asked, with a frown spreading across his face. I guess he wanted a quick interaction and hadn't prepared for a negotiation.

'It's my first day travelling and in my bag is my camera. I need this to take photos of my trip. I can't give it to you, sorry.'

He was even more confused by this answer, but seemed to accept it, moving on to notice that I had something in my pocket 'Well, what about that?' he said, pointing at my friend's mobile phone bulging out of my hip pocket.

'It's not mine to give. You can't have it.'

Realising that I wasn't going to hand over anything, he thrust the handle of the knife in his mouth and went to grab the strap of my bag with the intention to forcefully take my possessions. In that moment, as he leaned forward to grab my bag strap, I twisted around and, with one flowing move, I took the knife from his mouth. Within a few short seconds our dynamic had reversed and I was now standing in front of him, holding the knife, and he, eyes wide with shock, was staring at me, hands partly lifted in the air.

Behind me, the traffic had calmed down, and I had a small window for escaping this scene. Throwing the knife into a bush, I ran across the six lanes of traffic and stood watching the man pace to and fro frustratingly watching me through the sea of vehicles.

I had freed myself from a potential robbery, but had also cut myself off from the only route I knew back to the museum and safety with my friend.

The longer I live, the more I think that life is a paradox. It's healthy to learn from past mistakes, but unhealthy to allow past experiences to impact our decisions if it will limit our growth. My immediate experience taught me that strangers are dangerous, and yet, for me to find my way home, I had to rely on a new stranger to help me return to safety.

I had no choice but to believe that not all strangers wielded a knife or sinister thoughts around foreigners in a foreign city.

As the seconds passed, I could feel my chest tightening as I realised that the moment there was another pause in traffic, the man would cross over the road to pursue his hunger for my possessions. I didn't want to discover if he was as nervous about using his knife as before.

Desperate to find a quick way to move me far from this threat, I instinctively stuck out my thumb and generally waved at traffic, hoping that someone, preferably a wholesome family on the way to take their children to the same museum I was heading to, would take pity on me and stop.

The splutter of a motorbike jolted me out of my daydream and stopped in front of me was a leather-clad bearded man straddling a Harley-Davidson. He slipped off his helmet and passed it to me.

'A donde?' - where to, he asked.

'The museum,' I said, awkwardly thrusting the paper map towards him as I tried to point with the helmet I now held in my other hand.

Silently nodding, he tilted his head towards the rear of the Harley, gesturing for me to hop on the back. Jumping on the back of the motorbike, I instinctively wrapped my arms around his waist as he pulled off, yet quickly let go, thinking that it was wiser to loosely grip his leather waistcoat rather than pull me closer to his body.

Looking left, I could see the knife-man, arms limp to his side, dejectedly watching me as I rode by. Smirking, I silently congratulated myself for getting out of that awkward situation and relaxed into enjoying the warm breeze of Mexico City from the back of a Harley-Davidson.

The road was polka dotted with dozens of locals congregating at poles with cardboard signs I could only assume were makeshift bus stops. Some people were wearing brightly coloured traditional clothes, the same patterns depicting people from the same community clustering together, while other men, women and children carried boxes of sickly sweet smelling bags of, what I imagined to be, an exotic local delicacy.

Minibuses would pull up alongside these stops: the bus already spilling inside out with passengers and a flurry of exchange would take place; people would squeeze out of the bus with another body quickly filling the vacant gap.

Driving in Mexico City is a completely different experience to what I had ever experienced back in Europe. Having driven from Wales to Naples, in Italy, I thought that I was accustomed to wild and wonderful driving techniques. Yet Mexico appeared to take the erratic up another level. In addition to this being my first ever experience on Mexican roads, I was also riding shotgun on a Harley, whose rider paid little regard to traffic lights, stop signs, or even the police. 'Was I riding on the bike of a drug lord?' I mused.

After a few minutes, my calm curiosity dampened as I realised that my vantage point of viewing the city was maybe not the safest place to observe. Who was my saviour? And where in fact were we going? The act of him offering me his only helmet had given me a sense of security and trust in him that I was now questioning.

Not being able to speak to him, nor fully knowing where we were, my situation of being trapped on a moving bike and being driving to who knows where became my all consuming thought.

The year was 2002. This was long before GPS tracking or smartphones existed. The mobile device I was carrying only received calls - I didn't know anyone's number, or the local police number if I had to call for help. I suddenly felt really trapped and quite nervous.

'Breathe, Kate. Don't let it show,' I said to myself, realising that my grip had tightened on Harley-man's jacket. I didn't want him to know that I was afraid, I wanted to keep the thin air of illusion that I was in control and knew what I was doing. Looking back, I was a naive 23 year old, barely a woman, whose ignorance thought that she could ever be a match for a middle-aged, muscle-bound biker if he did decide to take advantage of this situation.

My mind whirled as I contemplated different scenarios when the bike did eventually stop. We might end up at his gang's garage, where a group of other burly, intense men would be waiting for me, and I would become their sex slave. After a few weeks of silence, my parents, increasingly concerned, would fly over and spend the rest of their lives desperately seeking for their only daughter, who was never to be seen again. We may end up weaving towards a mansion on top of a hill overlooking the city. As the gates open, I'd see a tiger swimming in a pool behind a metal fence, and armed guards surveying the bike and my arrival. He would turn to me, explaining that he is the son of the wealthiest drug lord in Mexico and heir to this realm. His father was recently shot by a rival gang, and to avoid future bloodshed, he struck a deal with them: He would surrender his territories in return for the safety of his and his employees' lives. Turning to me, he would then ask for my hand in marriage and ask for my help in building a new empire, using the money to give back to the city that he was proud to call home.

There was also the small chance that he was also riding to the museum, where my friend would be waiting for me and I could nonchalantly get off the bike, throwing him his helmet with a casual 'gracias,' while my friend would stare in awe at how cool - or probably ridiculously stupid and lucky - I was.

Knowing that my role for this part of the narrative was outside of my control, I decided to focus on the goodness of this person and believe that we were in fact heading to the museum. Why not believe that the future is good, rather than adding layers of unnecessary anxiety and stress prematurely. When, or if, I arrived at the dark garage with his biker friends, I'd need this spent nervous energy to try and run away, so better conserve it while I still could!

In what felt like an eternity, but was probably less than fifteen minutes, the bike slowed to a stop. Engine idling, I could see the grand pillars of the museum entrance and, with so much joy and relief, I hugged the rider, clunking his head with his own helmet that I was still wearing. 'Whoops, sorry!' I said, scrabbling off the bike as he rubbed the back of his head. 'Gracias so much, gracias!' I shouted and kept shouting as I ran to the safety of the museum entrance.

My friend was running late, and I thought it best to keep my story to myself, so when she arrived, pushing her sleeping 8-month old son in a pram, we had a calm and pleasant visit learning about the history of Mexico and its people.

'I hope you enjoyed your first day in Mexico,' she asked through a car window as she dropped me off at my accommodation.

'Oh yes, I learnt so much, thank you.' 'More than I could ever imagine,' I added to myself.

With only one day out of 365 down, it was obvious to all, myself included, that I had to reduce - preferably completely remove - any possible future harm, theft, or worse during my travels, but not at the cost of diluting my awe and curiosity. It would be a fine balance, but I was confident that I could find a way. There was no logical method I could use, so I decided to listen to my body. Any time I felt uncomfortable, or uneasy, I would immediately return to a safe space, regardless of where I was or who I was with.

This reconnection to my intuition, and trusting my gut instincts, served me well with only one more mishap, where just six weeks later, I almost get arrested for a murder I didn't commit, but this was more driven by the Mexican police fabricating a story to try and extract money from 'another foreigner' and I was the easiest scapegoat. Thanks to my poor Spanish, I accidentally used the slang word for 'cash' while desperately trying to rationalise with the policeman that no person had died, nor had I done anything to merit this attention.

'Please, let me get my documents and we can sort this out,' is what I wanted to say, while standing next to the van I had been driving en route to a dive site where I was working as a Divemaster. My guests, who were with me in the van and also witnessed a local car clipping the rear wheel of a cyclist while sneaking through a stop sign, had taken the female cyclist to hospital, as she had broken her collarbone. I naively stayed at the scene of the accident to give a witness statement.

The driver of the black SUV, still in his car (I assume it was a male, though I don't know for sure), quickly sped off as soon as the cyclist started moving from the floor. I later learnt that he had driven to the police station and paid them to make the problem (accident) someone else's. I was that someone else.

'Look, I am not near to where the accident took place,' I kept saying to a policeman, who appeared more interested in staring at my breasts than listening to me.

'We have witnesses,' he said to my cleavage, pointing in the general direction of a few houses that lined the road. I glanced over, noticing doors quietly being closed and curtains shimmering as the occupants secretly watched from afar, 'plus the cyclist is now dead, because you intentionally drove into him.'

'No, this is a lie!' I adamantly said, knowing that the cyclist had only suffered a broken collarbone and was otherwise fine. I was getting more and more desperate to remember some more Spanish words to better explain what transpired.

'I'll get my documents, and we can speak to the embassy, okay?'

Relief washed over the policeman's face. 'Vale, si.' Unbeknown to me, the Spanish slang word for cash is also what I had accidentally used for documents: 'papeles', papers is cash as well as documents. Fate was smiling down on me, otherwise I might have spent the weekend sitting in a Mexican cell wearing only a bikini top and cut-off jean shorts.

Relieved, I started to walk away, as the policeman had kept my work-van keys. Within a few hundred metres, a local friend of mine came over after checking that he was out of sight from the police. In hushed tones, he handed me a rucksack and said 'here's some clothes to change into, your passport and I also bought you a bus ticket to Belize. You need to leave now.'

Fear gripped me. 'But, why?' I said, stammering and struggling to comprehend what was happening.

'They will lock you up in prison until you pay a lot of money. You're a gringa, a foreigner, and it could take weeks before they inform your consulate. Better to go now.'

Barely holding back tears, I threw on a t-shirt and bandanna over my hair. The bus was already at the stop, and within a few minutes of me boarding the coach we pulled off. My friend waved goodbye and I bit my lip, promising to not cry until I crossed the Mexican border.

The bus trip took six hours, but it felt like an eternity of hyper-vigilance and raw emotions every single time the bus slowed or stopped. I was petrified that the police were following me and they would drag me off to the nearest station, where I would be found guilty of fleeing a crime scene as well as facing a completely fake murder charge.

Before leaving, my friend had whispered an address of their friend that could house me until I could arrange the rest of my belongings to be sent down from Mexico. He had loaned me a few days' worth of cash, assuring me that the dive company I worked for could refund him from the salary they owed me. His cash gift was the only money I had as my debit card was still in my bag in the room I rented in the hostel.

He had warned me, 'Do not write the address down. If you are caught, I don't want the police to know who is helping you.' For six long hours, I repeated the mantra of the safe address '36 Rosewood Street, 36 Rosewood Street.' I had to remember it, otherwise I had no idea what would happen to me when I eventually arrived in Belize City.

We finally crossed the border, and with a huge sigh of relief, I burst into tears. Finally I could relax a bit. The Mexican police couldn't chase me into Belize and, even though I was only travelling with the clothes I had on my back, I was alive and free!

Arriving at the destination of Belize City at night, it already felt different to the sleepy Mexican coastal village of Tulum that I had come from. The air was sticky and there was an earthy, almost pungent, smell that coated my nostrils. The other passengers scattered into the night, and I was left alone in a dimly lit tin shack with only the tip of a distant cigarette nearby to alert me that others were present. Still rattled from my police encounter, I was very wary of 'strangers', especially being in such a vulnerable position of being alone with barely anyone knowing where I was.

Slumping on a local bench constructed of a piece of wood balanced across a few empty milk crates, I closed my eyes and focused on my breathing. I needed to be in the moment and feel if the situation was safe, or if I was still living with my fear from what had happened earlier. Breathe. The knot in my stomach started to undo, and slowly I started to feel more me.

Gently opening my eyes, I looked around. I could make out a silhouette of a few people, where I had first seen the glowing tip of the cigarette.

'Do I trust them?' I asked myself. Looking around, I saw that we were the only people left in the shack, so this question was a moot point. I either stayed in the makeshift bus shack alone all night, risking being exposed to whoever and whatever happens in this city with nowhere to run to, or I asked for help from these strangers.

I chose the latter. Fortunately for me, Belize is an English-speaking country, so as I rolled my shoulders back, slowly walking towards the group of four 20 something young men, I tried to look as confident and in control as possible. I wanted to portray that I had options, I was choosing to speak with them because I could. I was a woman travelling the world and had it all together, not a lost little girl far from home and desperately needing help.

'Hi guys,' I gushed, flashing a big smile and casually holding my bag on one shoulder. 'Was wondering if you could point me to Rosewood Street, gonna meet a friend there,' I lied. I wanted them to know they couldn't do anything to me as I was expected somewhere by people.

'Where?' The guy closest to me asked, flicking his cigarette but on the floor, absently twisting it out with the toe of his shoe.

'Rosewood Street?' I replied, a little less confident than before.

'Never heard of it,' was his reply, along with murmurs of agreement from the others.

That was all I needed to hear and the overwhelming events of the day engulfed me as tears started falling from my eyes. 'Oh,' I meagrely replied, quickly looking down and trying to wipe the tears away before they noticed.

'Problems with the Mexican police?' one asked a few moments later. I looked up, surprised that they guessed, expecting them to be laughing at me, or rubbing their hands together sinisterly as they plotted how to take advantage of this situation, but all I was met with was sympathetic looks and nods of support.

'My aunty lives nearby. You can stay with her until you get sorted. Come,' he said, gesturing to a car parked on the other side of the road. I scanned the group, and every single one was looking at me sympathetically. I decided that I could trust them, partly because I had no one else to believe and partly because if they were wicked men about to take advantage of me, and I didn't go with them, all they had to do was wait a few hours and complete their sinister activities on me when I fell asleep at the bus stop. Better to get it over and done with, I rationalised.

The five of us squeezed into the car and drove to a two-storey wooden house. As the door opened, a woman wearing a bright blue floral dress with a bright red apron tied around her waist filled the doorframe.

'Hello my dear, you must be tired and hungry,' warmly ushering me indoors while simultaneously waving her nephew and friends away. 'This will be your room, and I'll bring you some fry jacks and plantain shortly. You'll be starving after all that travel,' I nodded in agreement.

Belly full and finally safe, I fell into a deep and dreamless sleep. The next few days reaffirmed my belief that most strangers are inherently good, for the 'youths' who had helped me at the bus stop lent me a bicycle so I could explore the city, and they also arranged with all the market stall owners to let me eat and buy replacement clothes on credit. Within a few days, most people had heard of the foreign woman who had fled from the Mexican police and generously offered me an abundance of hospitality. 'Hey chica,' they shouted as I cycled past their stall, 'join us for some mango.' Most days, I was found sitting on the side of the road, drinking freshly squeezed orange juice and playing cards with another new friend. All the while my bag, clothes and other possessions I had abandoned in Mexico slowly trickled in as other travellers coming from Tulum to Belize carried random items with them.

I couldn't have asked for a better experience to rekindle my passion for travelling and, after almost two weeks of living with the lady I affectionately called 'Aunty', I felt it time for me to continue south towards other lands and adventures.

Even though I never had another high-risk or fear-inducing experience, one chance encounter with a girl, called Katie, would change my life forever.

Katie not only shared a similar name to me, but also reminded me of myself in many ways. She was tall, athletic, and also had long, blond hair. Yet, what she had that I felt I was missing was a deep sense of awareness of who she was in the world. This grounding confidence was attractive, and I envied her assurance of wanting to move to New Zealand to study Oceanography. I wished that I had her vision for my own life, because as the days of my year of travelling ticked by, I was noticing I still had no idea what I was going to do once I boarded my final flight home.

While in Guatemala, Katie invited me to climb a volcano to watch the sunrise, and I readily agreed. Only holding a hand-drawn map of the path to the summit, and carrying enough food and water for 24 hours, we started trekking towards the summit. Assuming that the best path was just walking in a straight line uphill, we ignored the map and quickly got lost, weaving through dense forests and through farmland and being chased by dogs until we had to jump over a fence, separating us from the protective and quite aggressive canines. As the sun set, we camped under a tree, hugging each other to keep warm and ate cold pasta and frijoles that we brought in a small plastic bag. Having no light with us, we fell asleep as it turned to night, awaking a few hours later surprisingly warm and still shrouded in darkness.

Putting away our makeshift camp, we hiked the remaining few kilometres to reach the basin of the largest volcano I had ever seen, just as the sun started to peek out above the horizon. As the sun slowly lifted, lighting layers of this exotic country in front of us, we were awed into silence at the majestic beauty of our planet. The moment felt magical and, being at the highest peak, brought a significance to our actions and words. We wasted no energy on small talk, preferring to sit in silence and absorb the day waking up around us. I gently wiggled my bare toes in my shoes, trying to warm them as I had placed my socks on my hands as makeshift gloves.

Gently, and with an air of conviction, in her voice, Katie said 'When I get to New Zealand I'm going to do an Ironman triathlon. There was no doubt in her voice, and she spoke as if it had already happened. I had confidence that her statement was as good as a fact, coupled with the magic that anything uttered on this volcano peak would come true.

I had never heard of Ironman before this moment, and after she informed me of the trilogy of sports and distances required to complete back-to-back, I could barely imagine how to finish one of the disciplines, let alone all three. I was in awe that she could even imagine swimming 2.4 miles (4.8 km), cycling 112 miles (180 km) to finish her Ironman with a 26.2 miles (42.2 km) marathon run, so I sat in silence.

Yet, even though Katie and I didn't keep in touch after our hike, her story of competing in a triathlon and my immense awe and near disbelief at the challenge of an Ironman stayed with me. The seed of becoming a triathlete had been planted. Almost 10 years later this volcano-peak conversation would reappear, and I would be ready to feed the dream of completing an Ironman. Yet back in Guatemala I was happy enough to watch the sunrise and joyously run back to the nearby city and onwards to live out the rest of my gap year.

My twelve months of travel passed within a blink of an eye. After leaving Central America, I hitchhiked my way through South America, Australasia and ended up in Thailand on a call with my mother just days before my final flight home. My round-the-world ticket expired after 364 days from my departure date, and still not knowing what I wanted to do, or where I wanted to live, I had called my mother to ask her advice on whether I should extend my trip as I had just been offered a job as a Western Geisha in Japan.

'Absolutely not,' was the advice I received. My mother, missing me terribly, refused to entertain extending my trip, and my desire to be a 'good daughter' overruled my passion for travel, so I boarded my final flight back to Britain.

Drifting with the clouds

'Oh darling, we've missed you,' my mother cooed in between hugs. My parents had driven to meet me at Heathrow Airport and welcome me back, and I was being pulled between my Mum's and Dad's embraces, and neither were letting me go, maybe for fear I'd turn on my heel and catch another flight out of there!

After mopping our tears of joy for seeing each other again, we loaded my one bag into the car and headed back to the same house in the same town I'd called home for most of my life. Returning home was, strangely, a cultural shock. Even though I was returning 'home' to my country of birth, I felt disconnected to the reserved and tame culture that I had left. I craved the bright colours, the potent scents and noisy crowds that had consumed my journey. My eyes scanned the horizons for ragged peaks tempting me to climb, but instead all I saw were the gentle rolling green hills of Wales.

Not much had changed in the past year. It was still raining, and the winter clouds made the house seem that bit darker than I recalled.

In honour of my return, my mother had prepared my favourite meal as a 'welcome home' present. Sitting down at the kitchen table, I took a bite of the lovingly prepared dish. As I bit into what I knew I used to love, I almost spat the mouthful out, finding it tough and bland. Seeing my parents both enjoying the meal, I knew it wasn't the food, but me.

Even though I looked the same, something had fundamentally shifted within me. Not only was I looking at things anew, my palate had altered and I craved the exotic spices and heat of Latin America. I wanted vibrant colours and explosions of taste and flavour not just on my tongue, but in my life! Looking at my parents across the table, they seemed oblivious to this fire burning within me. They wanted me to start looking for a job and 'settle down'. As I was surveying the familiar yet alien room, I realised that my father had been talking for quite a while '...and we've been doing some research and found some very interesting jobs for you. Of course, you need to justify this year off, but they should be lenient thanks to your high grades....' I decided to switch off again. All this talk of conforming was overwhelming me and I could feel my chest tightening and heart start racing at the thought of becoming normalised.

The week drifted into a month and I kept busy with long walks and trips to the local library to avoid the conversation of a job, or my future. For my five years in university, I had a focus and an outcome I needed to achieve. And that goal was for my freedom to travel. Once I was travelling I had kinda lost my direction. Yes, I was on an exploration of the world and myself, but I was also floating wherever the wind blew me. I was free to meander with no agenda and go wherever I wanted.

Now that this year - my dream - had been fulfilled, I hadn't planned what was coming next, and being back in my childhood bedroom, sleeping in a single bed and surrounded with far too many stuffed toys for any one child, I was acutely aware of my reality.

I'd had my year of fun and adventure. Was now the time to start getting real and serious about my present and future?

It's curious that the older we get, the more serious we 'should' be taking life. The words 'get serious' and 'settle down' always sound so heavy and dull. Why do we need to take life seriously? Can't we keep smiling and laughing throughout every stage of our life?

Yet, we do seem to start removing moments of silliness and fun, replacing them with significant and heavy decisions. Things like a mortgage, starting a pension, and if our shoes match our bag seem to play a larger role than enjoying the moment.

In my heart, I thought it was possible to have fun doing what I loved and creating an income and means to support myself… but my mother's words haunted me in these moments. 'Your head is in the clouds, Kate.' Maybe, I was wrong and I needed to stop drifting and start being responsible.

Reluctantly, I applied for, and was offered, a job in a local engineering firm. The company supplied machines to aeroplane and satellite manufacturers globally and, because I was the only employee who spoke more than one language, my job offered a small opportunity for me to travel while attending European trade shows. I enjoyed learning about aeroplane manufacture, yet struggled enormously with the rigid working hours of 8am start and 5pm finish, with one hour for lunch. My body and brain preferred to flow when I felt creative and productive, rather than the rigid set of rules for when I need to be working, exercising or resting. I had to fight against my natural rhythms and force myself to conform and fit in.

Again, I fully immersed myself into my situation, rationalising that if I was going to live a Monday to Friday lifestyle, then I would live it to the fullest, and as soon as I was eligible, I applied for a mortgage, bought a new-build suburban house and also started dating a colleague at work. There was still a small stubborn part of me that refused to wholly forget everything from my trip, so I also entered an Ironman 70.3 triathlon, a half Ironman distance. Not competent in juggling work, the immense fatigue I felt from the rigid work hours, as well as buying a new home and new relationship, my training for my first ever triathlon was sporadic at best.

On the day of the race, I struggled through the 1.2 mile swim, grew tireder and tireder on the 56 mile cycle and for the 13.1 mile run, I think I walked most of it and could feel my leg muscles tightening with every stride. Dragging myself across the finish line while clutching my side to ease the pain from a stomach cramp, I found a little patch of grass, sat down and cried. Tears of relief from having finished, anger for having taken for granted the enormity of the race and also shock that I was getting closer to completing an Ironman dream that had started to consume me.

My boyfriend, let's call him Geraint, had surprised me and driven down to watch the race even though I had asked him not to. I wanted time alone to process what was my next step with this new sport, as well as a wider picture of my life and career.

'Well done, Kate,' Geraint said, as I crawled on my hands and knees into the car, wishing that I hadn't sat down at the end of the race as my legs had immediately seized and walking was no longer an option.

'Now that you've done this, you don't need to do any more triathlons, do you?' He said, posing more a statement than a question. I was tired, drained from all energy, in quite a bit of physical pain and had nothing to push back with. And, so I agreed, with a meek 'OK.' And, just like that, I gave up on my dream of ever completing an Ironman.

Once I was able to stand up from a chair without groaning from muscle fatigue, I slowly started returning to the gym and even joined an evening kickboxing class. One evening when Geraint was staying over, which was becoming more frequent, as I was getting changed into my gym clothes, I could hear from the kitchen a pop of a cork being pulled from a bottle of wine and Geraint shouting 'I miss you when you go out... why not stay in and watch TV with me tonight?'

Looking back, I cringe at the many times I last-minute cancelled a gym class, or let down a friend I was meeting because Geraint said he'd miss me, or that I didn't need to go to the gym because I was more beautiful without muscles, but back then I thought that it was sweet and loving how he wanted to spend so much time with me. Yet, gradually and over many years, this sweetness and desire to be with me was replaced with a controlling and desperate need to know where I was at every time of the day and night.

But, I'm getting a bit ahead of myself.

Now that I had a house, a job and a boyfriend, my societal 'tick-box lifestyle' was exactly what was expected of me, and very predictable. The groundhog day experience of my life was slowly suffocating me and I still believed that I couldn't change my job unless I knew what I was changing it for - because isn't having certainty with a mediocre job better than the uncertainty of following our passion?

Geraint and I drifted into months and then years of being together. I was, again, comfortable. Work wasn't demanding and I had a safe and secure lifestyle that allowed me to not worry about the small comforts of life.

To quench my desire to give back, I started donating money to a charity, ensuring that my security also benefited others. It felt a good thing to do: a comfortable way of helping others.

I didn't get the same 'feel good' feeling as I did while travelling and organically supporting locals, such as Maria and her family living in a small mountain village in Guatemala. An impromptu bus trip to Todos Santos and getting lost after a mountain walk forced me to ask for directions from a lady grinding corn in her front garden. Her name was Maria and after this brief encounter, I moved in with her and her 4 children for a month. Paying her five dollars a day and taking her two youngest children to a local bookshop each week, she taught me how to prepare tortillas from hand-grinding corn, how to wash clothes on the large rocks next to a local river, and, while sitting on the cold concrete floor in a corner of her garden, she taught me how build my own loom and weave.

In return for her generosity, I helped promote Maria to other tourists, and it wasn't before long that Maria was selling her hand-woven belts and tops, as well as hosting weaving classes for other travellers. Donating money didn't give me the same sense of connection that I had experienced working alongside Maria, but I felt good that I was doing something.

Back in Wales, the evenings when Geraint was travelling abroad with work, I would read motivational books and autobiographies of game-changing people. People who stepped away from their circumstances to create a life they wanted to live. Some of these biographies shared how they felt compelled to right an injustice in the world while others were drawn to the sweetness of a better life for themselves.

It was during these evenings, when I was able to surround myself with imaginary mentors and guides, showing to me that maybe, just maybe, my desire to step away from the normal way of living wasn't that crazy after all.

When Geraint came home from his travels, he returned full of stories about trends happening in the USA, of what people bought in

Japan, and how the culture in the Middle East was now impacting business. I was living vicariously through him.

Being in a couple, and not knowing any differently (or better), I assumed we needed to do everything together and I couldn't deviate from what he wanted to do, regardless of my personal wishes. As traditional as it sounds, all the couples in my life operated as one unit and did most things together. They completed, not complimented, each others' lives.

Even though we weren't married, with Geraint, I saw us as one, and for every aspect of 'us', I made sure that we faced the same direction, even if it meant me stepping away from some things I wanted to do.

So, when Geraint returned one evening and announced he wanted to move to Australia, I didn't see I had a place to object. The decision had been made, we were emigrating to Oz, with Geraint being sponsored through a job he had found, and me coming along on a 'de facto spouse' visa - in the eyes of Australian law, we were as good as married, and I was tied to him, through our visa, if I wanted to stay in the country.

While Geraint was obliged under the regulations surrounding his Australian visa to work for the same company, I had the freedom to do what I wanted. Curious about setting up my own business, and Geraint having seen first-hand the growth of franchises in America, we decided to purchase a food franchise in the suburb we were living, with the intention to open my own independent shop a little while later.

Within a few months, I was the proud manager and owner of a Subway franchise 15 minutes' walk away from home, and I threw myself into being the perfect franchisee and boss. Working 6 days a week and being on-call for the seventh, I slowly grew the business to a level I could sell it for a profit but not without a cost to me. I made no time for myself, barely made any friends, and still didn't know what my personal desires or goals were. I no longer had time to even consider training to complete a full Ironman triathlon, and I rationalised this decision, promising that 'when I have more time, and money, I'll then start training'. Being a good partner to Geraint and growing my business were the only two considerations I had.

I was focusing so hard on what Geraint wanted, I lost touch with what I wanted and loved. I was drifting through life, being pulled in directions that weren't displeasing, just not where I wanted to be. I had a spark, that fire to fuel change, but no direction to shoot at.

And, again, my life was comfortable, with a fun job, a standard relationship, and an average life living in suburban Australia. We had money to afford simple luxuries of occasional dinners out and, again, I had no real pain to fight against. To anyone looking at my life, I was 'successful', but it wasn't my kind of success.

I knew I didn't want this life, but never asked what I wanted instead.

As per the plan, within a few years, we sold the Subway franchise and decided to fulfil one of Geraint's dreams; to own a guesthouse.

I was focusing so much on keeping other people happy, I had forgotten what made me smile. I had closed down sharing what I truly thought and felt, focusing instead on completing the image of being happy.

By automatically answering 'I'm fine, everything's good with me,' I had slowly creeped into a place where I thought that everything was fine, that I was living the life I wanted and the moments of sadness and 'what if', I put down to a typical side effect of life.

In August of 2008, needing sell my house in Wales and borrowing a bridging loan from my parents, Geraint and I over-leveraged ourselves financially to fulfil on one of his dreams: We exchanged on a dilapidated, dusty and old building in rural Australia with the intention to open a guesthouse. This happened at the same time as Geraint secured Permanent Residency, freeing him from his engineering job and enabling him to work alongside me in our business.

The guesthouse was above our budget, and we maxed out every line of credit, including a few credit cards to cover some expenses, but I was on a mission to not say 'no' to Geraint. He wanted to fulfil his dream of owning a guesthouse, and I was on a misguided mission to make sure he was happy and that I didn't fail him.

We opened our guesthouse and restaurant and, for the first few months, we both worked seven days a week renovating and preparing for our grand opening to the public. Our plan was that Geraint would be responsible for the seven guest rooms and I would be in charge of our 65-seater restaurant. Within days, Geraint was struggling to greet the guests and clean the rooms. He was starting to show signs of anxiety when, on the rare occasion, one of our guests complained, even if it was just that the coffee he had served was too hot.

'Kate, I can't do this any more,' he announced, throwing his apron to the back of the kitchen.

It was 8:30 am, and I had only slept four hours after a long evening shift serving tables and washing plates in our restaurant. Wanting to support him, I had offered to wake up early and help Geraint prepare the guests' breakfasts.

This very instant, I didn't need Geraint's increasingly frequent dramas of pretend-quitting. We were barely breaking even and I desperately needed Geraint to dig deeper and push through the fatigue. We were in this together, feeling the short-term pain of starting a hospitality business, and I personally felt that he wasn't thinking about what was best for our business and our future, and was exclusively focusing on his needs.

I could feel my whole body tense as I turned to face him.

'This was your idea to buy the guesthouse. What did you expect? That it'd be a walk in the park?'

I immediately regretted what I said. Geraint was very sensitive and I had no idea how my curt response would be taken. I felt guilty that I was so harsh on him. He was working to the best of his ability and maybe I could support him more?

'Look, I'm sorry.' I said, backtracking from my reactive reply, 'I didn't mean to snap. I'm tired and struggling too. How about I work the weekend breakfast shift alone and you can lie-in?'

'Well yeah, I need more time off, so it's a start.'

Walking past his crumpled apron on a nearby workbench, he returned to our bedroom. I wasn't sure how I could serve fourteen guests by myself, but I knew I'd give it my best shot.

That was the last day Geraint ever helped with breakfast, and while Geraint lay in bed downstairs, I needed to step up my game and learn how to be an efficient waitress, breakfast cook, coffee maker, and all this without my guests realising that I was doing it alone.

The distance between the guests' tables and the coffee machine was 15 metres and the kitchen was half way between the two. It was going to be a hard request to make sure I didn't burn the breakfast while I made the coffee or neglect my guests while I was dashing around making the food.

Tough as it was, I managed to find a rhythm and flow to serving the guests alone, and the initially stressful scenario became routine within a few short weeks. I started to set myself little challenges to see how many people I could serve at once. The challenges were silly, but it helped feed my pretence that I was enjoying my lifestyle. If only for a few short minutes, I could laugh as I tried to poach 8 eggs simultaneously. I was learning new skills and distracting myself from the resentment towards work and Geraint that was slowly building up in me.

Over time, the number of hours Geraint worked in our business slowly decreased until he stopped working all together. For weeks, he would sit downstairs watching TV as I was on my hands and knees scrubbing the guest bathrooms or chopping wood for the fire.

In the afternoons, he'd meander up the street to a local cafe, enjoying a chat with a friend over a coffee and slice of cake. I couldn't leave the guesthouse to join them as we had bookings most days and someone needed to be in the property to greet them.

I started to feel like a prisoner in my own home. I rarely left the property, and when I did I still had to answer phone calls and be 'on call' for guests, I was trapped in a 24 hours-a-day life that I didn't really want to be living.

After a few months of Geraint lurking around the house and not helping with the running of the business, we decided he needed to get a job and start contributing financially. It would've made more sense for me to leave the property and work, because I had the engineering degrees and could earn more money, but Geraint was adamant that he wanted nothing more to do with the guesthouse.

Back in the UK, I had briefly worked in a recruitment office, so had experience on how to spice up resumes, and one evening I sat down and helped Geraint apply for positions as an engineer. He had experience and good references, but no qualifications to back it up.

Eventually, he got a job in Sydney, 3 hours' drive away from home. He'd be travelling around the country selling electrical devices for a family-run engineering firm. The money was much needed, but it meant he would be away from home for weeks at a time.

I didn't know if I'd miss him, but decided to keep this thought to myself.

Months passed with only the colour of the leaves in the garden serving as a reminder to the passing of time. My days blurred into one long, mundane memory. I had not only lost my desire for something more in my life, a purpose, I'd also lost the desire to search for one.

As I made beds, cleaned bathrooms and prepared coffees, I didn't have the space to reflect, to dream and to wish. It was as if I was on autopilot, drifting through life waiting for something to happen to me, to wake me up from this dreamless life.

As the years passed, I increasingly found myself not saying 'no' to Geraint. If we shared opposing viewpoints, or if he wanted to do something I didn't, his reaction felt more extreme than required. So I gradually stopped saying 'no' to him altogether, even doing things I didn't want to. I justified it by telling myself, 'Someone has to compromise, why not me? I'm broadening my shoulders to carry bigger burdens.'

Sometimes they were small requests such as me walking to the local newsagents' and buying a newspaper while he stayed in bed. Other times, they were a lot bigger.

On Saturday 18 February 2012, I had a long overdue wake-up call.

Every year, Geraint returned back to the UK to see his family and catch-up with friends. I wasn't allowed this luxury because I had to work in the guesthouse: Geraint wouldn't cover my shifts and I couldn't justify the expense of paying someone to work in my place because our business was still repaying our initial loans.

Geraint had just returned from one such trip, and as I carried the last of the breakfast plates into the kitchen after a busy morning I almost dropped them in surprise because he was sitting at the back of the kitchen.

'Why are you here? Is there something wrong?'

Stumbling, I clumsily put the plates down and anxiously went over to see Geraint.

'Nothing's wrong. Just wanted to see you.'

This wasn't typical behaviour. I couldn't remember the last time Geraint had been upstairs while guests were around. I was on-guard and didn't know how to respond, nervously biting my lower lip and hiding my hands in the pockets of my shorts.

'I thought we could go for a picnic. Can you go and buy some sandwiches for us?'

Geraint rarely liked me leaving the guesthouse. Even when he was working in the city, he'd regularly call to make sure I was in the building and hadn't gone out, loosely disguising his surveillance as 'miss you, what are you doing?'

Him inviting me to leave the property on one of the busiest days of the week - a Saturday - was out of the norm to say the least.

'I'd love to, but I'm really busy and have people arriving in a few hours...'

It didn't sit well with me that he was acting so different to his usual self. Of course, I wanted to sit under a tree and enjoy the warm summer sun, but after many years of us living together and me running the guesthouse, his offer seemed more like a test than a reward.

'Come on, you can clean the rooms when you get back.'

I had learnt that it was easier to say yes to Geraint than no. Since we had bought the guesthouse Geraint's anxiety and stress levels had increased dramatically, and the few times in the past I'd expressed a difference of opinion it usually ended in an argument. Today, I didn't want to fight and I was also looking forward to a walk, albeit a short one, in the beautiful blue gum forest that was just out of reach to me most of the time. 'OK, let's go,' I said, realising I'd been holding my breath as I left out a deep exhale.

As I collected some sandwiches from the local deli, Geraint drove his car and picked me up. Relaxing in the passenger seat, I watched as the view from my window changed from the town I knew so well to the blue-gum forest that surrounded us.

The paved road turned to gravel and we slowly climbed up a hill until the road ended next to a lookout.

Getting out of the car, I was met with a gush of intense dry and hot air. Australia's weather still surprised me, it was so different from the cool and damp climate of the UK.

Breathing in the warmth, I closed my eyes and felt the sun bite down on my face. It felt good to be outside, if only for a short while. My shoulders relaxed as I breathed in the deep smells of the Australian eucalyptus forest smells. It was exotic and uplifted me, giving me hope that maybe, just maybe, one day I would be able to change my circumstances and get out of my seven-day work routine.

Whispering quietly to myself, I repeated a sentence that kept me going on the days I wanted to give up: 'When you've got more time, then you can start living again. Just not today.'

Slowly opening my eyes, I turned around, expecting to see Geraint eating his sandwich under a nearby tree, but he wasn't. Kneeling in front of me, he looked up and asked me a question I thought I'd never hear, 'Kate, will you marry me?'

Fumbling in one of his pockets, he pulled out a ring I recognised immediately. It was the same ring I had been playing with since I was a little girl. As a child, I'd sneak into my parents' bedroom, and while my mother was getting changed I'd sit at her dresser and pretend to be her while brushing my hair and putting on her jewellery.

The ring Geraint was holding was a ring my father had bought my mother - it was her engagement ring.

The colour drained from my face and I started to tremble involuntarily. This shouldn't be happening. We weren't happy enough to commit to *forever*.

Over the past few years, it felt like Geraint and I had been slowly disconnecting. We spent more time apart than together, and on the few occasions we were in the same room, our conversation focused on television programs and whether we'd drink a bottle of red or white wine with dinner. Over the past few years, I could count on one hand the number of times we had been intimate with each other, with both of us using tiredness as an excuse. On the rare occasion Geraint was determined to be amorous, I'd cook a big meal and make sure we drank lots of alcohol to hopefully numb him from his amorous advances, mostly for fear of him forcing me to do things that I found uncomfortable, or hurt me.

He wanted to commit to this loveless, sexless relationship forever?!

Geraint started fidgeting, and sensing his nerves, tears sprung to my eyes. I looked down at my mother's ring and guessed what she wanted me to do.

Geraint and I still owed my parents some money we had borrowed to buy the guesthouse, and I took this ring as a symbol to honour our debt - my obligation to my family and also the years I'd spent with this man.

Nine years is a long time to be with someone; it's hard to start over again, older, with more baggage, more wrinkles and a little less sparkle in my eyes. There would also be the debt I knew I'd have to carry alone if I didn't marry Geraint, because there was no doubt in my mind that he would never honour what we owed my family.

Tears flowed down my cheeks as I nodded my head, locking myself to this man who I doubted knew how far from happy we both were.

Expressing more relief than joy, Geraint awkwardly stood up handing me the ring I knew so well. It fitted, though I didn't have to put it on my finger to know this.

'Well, we'd better get back to the guesthouse,' Geraint announced, dusting down his knees and preparing to drive me back to cleaning rooms for our guests.

Yes, life was the same. I was being driven back to our business for me to get on my hands and knees and continue scrubbing toilets. The only difference was I had just tied myself to this life forever.

That evening, I started drinking earlier than normal, I needed more alcohol than usual to process the day. Geraint was more than happy to join me.

'There's no point in waiting, let's get married as quickly as possible. How about December?'

Just for tonight, I just wanted to forget the engagement, but Geraint was persistent in choosing a date.

'There's no rush, let's just repay our debt and start with a clean slate,' I partly pleaded, hoping that I could drag out a long engagement while we sorted out our finances.

Looking back, I feel ashamed that, due to my inability to be honest, I lied to both Geraint and myself. I was consumed by guilt for not being able to repay my parents, feeling as if I had failed to meet their expectations. In my thirties, I was in debt, struggling in a relationship with a man who tracked my every move and monitored our joint bank account. I couldn't bear adding more to this long list of failures, so remaining in a relationship became the only thing I desperately clung to, hoping that somehow I could encourage Geraint to be more supportive and a better partner for me.

Geraint was still talking away even though I had excused myself a few minutes' ago. It was as if he hadn't even realised I'd left the room. What a perfect evening to represent our relationship: Him doing his thing and me doing mine, without any need for interaction from the other… and I had agreed to being like this forever.

Forever.

That word hung over every single action.

Would I be watching hours of television every night, forever?

Would I be scared of expressing my opinion with my life partner, forever?

Was this what I'd signed up to?

'For fuck's sake Kate, yes or no?'

His raised voice brought me back physically and metaphorically to the room.

'Yes master, whatever you say,' I responded sarcastically.

This response had started off a joke one Sunday evening when Geraint had chastised me for forgetting to iron his work shirts.

'Damn it Kate, what am I supposed to wear to work tomorrow? What the hell have you been doing all day?'

Biting my tongue, I fought my desire to remind him that, for the past three days, he'd been lying in bed watching trash TV and texting me to bring him food and drink while I had worked ten-hours each day cooking breakfasts, cleaning rooms, greeting guests, and generally running our business single-handed.

Seeing his same flushed face on our engagement evening as on the other occasions, I knew that it wasn't worth my breath to snap back. I'd learnt that when I pushed back, Geraint would threaten to leave me and screw my family over by ignoring the money we owed them.

I could carry the personal attack, but the guilt of dragging my family down was too big for me to bear.

Mock-bowing to him, I gave up fighting. 'Yes master, I'm sorry master.'

Taking my words seriously, Geraint relaxed, relieved to know he was right and had proven me wrong. 'Good. Don't do it again.'

His voice snapped me back to the present. 'To our wedding in December, Kate!' he said, raising his glass in the air before taking a big gulp before I could reciprocate.

The knot in my stomach tightened and I suddenly felt nauseous, doubting it was the two bottles of wine we'd just finished that caused it.

Smiling with my mouth, but not my eyes, I reciprocated Geraint's 'cheers' and turned my attention on the television.

As the television droned on in the background, the enormity of the day washed over me.

I had pushed through these past few years expecting, or wishing, that something would change. But I'd never created the change. I was just drifting with the current, hoping that an external force would blow me on-course to something more fulfilling, more me.

Sitting in separate seats and in silence as we both sipped our glasses of wine watching drivel on the television, I saw decades of wasted time - wasted life - stretching out in front of me.

Was this the cliff-edge moment when a knight in shining armour would swoop in and save me from this mundane life? Geraint wasn't good for me, and I wasn't good for him either.

I decided to have as few sober moments as possible throughout our engagement. Geraint was travelling more due to work commitments, and I used the time alone to sample local wines under the pretence of choosing what we wanted for our wedding.

My best mate, Lydia, gladly stepped up as my drinking partner and spent many a happy evening singing 70s songs with me, using our hair brushes as microphones!

I adored these evenings when I could literally and metaphorically let my hair down. Invariably alcohol-fuelled, and not worried about the repercussions of Geraint judging me or clipping my wings, I spoke freely, I felt I could drop my guard down and just be me.

'Oh Lydia,' I sighed, arms outstretched and staring at the star-lit sky above me as we collapsed outside after a two-hour karaoke session, 'I don't know what on earth I want.'

Over yet another deep and meaningful evening over far too many glasses of wine, I found myself contemplating what other options I had, other than marrying Geraint.

In these moments I did feel guilty. Even though I never physically cheated on Geraint, by me questioning us being together felt like I was being unfaithful.

Geraint had rented a room in a house-share closer to his work and I knew he had a close relationship with a female who was also staying in the house. I never asked him how close they were, but the way his cheeks flushed when I mentioned her name made me question the innocence of their friendship.

Lying in my back-garden, drunk off wine with a girlfriend was so far from cheating, but entertaining the idea that I was making a mistake marrying Geraint was stepping over a line I wasn't yet prepared to cross.

'I know you think I'm making a mistake, but I have to think about my family. And the money we owe them.'

Lydia wasn't impressed with my logical analysis of my life - and especially not the decision that I had to marry Geraint.

'You're following your head, not your heart.'

Lydia, staring at the same sky I was, had a completely different perception of the life I'd committed to live.

And she had a point. Logic dictated for Geraint and I to stay together. With Geraint's salary and my hard work in our business, we could repay our debt gradually over the next ten years and start saving up for a comfortable retirement.

But my heart wasn't in it. If I was honest, I'd known for years that Geraint and I were together just because we had nothing better offered to us. He rarely touched me, preferring to get drunk and fall asleep in front of the television. And I preferred the nights when he did fall asleep and I went to bed alone.

It was a sad, but functioning and silent agreement we had created.

And with every day that passed, it drew our wedding one day closer.

In true Geraint-style, he relinquished all control over what happened on the day of our union, placing all decisions and responsibility on my shoulders.

I wanted the day to be perfect, to hide the fact that our relationship wasn't.

The week before the wedding, I couldn't sleep. Lying in a dark room, staring at the ceiling, I was troubled. Geraint was gently snoring next to me, oblivious that I'd been suffering from insomnia for many months.

Whenever I closed my eyes, the same dream would arrive. In my dream, I would awake in my bed, arching my back like a cat as my eyes slowly opened. Swinging my legs off the side of the bed, I'd slide my feet into glass slippers and walk into the lounge.

Standing around a small table, waiting for me, was my mother and a few close friends. As soon as I arrived, they guided me in front of a full-length mirror and my mother would slip a beautiful white gown on me while Lydia placed a vine of delicate flowers on my head.

Looking in the mirror, I'd see my father walk in behind me, proudly admiring his little daughter.

'You're doing the right thing,' he'd say as he gently kissed my forehead.

My dream would then jump to me arriving at the location for our wedding ceremony, a dramatic cliff lookout in the Blue Gum forest.

As my father helped me out of the car, two lines of friends, wearing brightly coloured dresses, hats, and suits, formed a pathway, leading me towards the celebrant and a dark figure standing next to her. The contrast of colour to the blue-green eucalyptus trees was breathtaking and I'd pause, feeling the joy of being surrounded by these majestic trees and dear friends.

Slowly, I would start to walk through the crowd of friends heading towards who I assumed to be Geraint, but I could never see the end of the aisle or his face.

With every step I took, I would feel heavier, forced to walk slower. And, as I pushed through this mental quicksand, the bright dresses of my friends would start fading, the colours being squeezed out and replaced by greys and blacks. The details of my friends' faces would blur, creating harsh jagged lines. And, increasingly, it was getting harder and harder to move forward.

As soon as I arrived at the end of the aisle, my dream would turn black and I'd awake with a gasp and covered in a cold sweat.

I had talked to Geraint about my concerns, that we were maybe marrying for the wrong reasons, but he discounted my apprehension as foolish and 'nothing to worry about'.

I felt that I couldn't talk to my parents. I was scared that they'd think I was abandoning them and not putting our family first. This was a crazy concoction I'd created in my head - and the only outcome it guaranteed was that I felt alone, and very scared.

The week before the wedding, Geraint and I had arranged a dinner with my parents and his mother, Sally, as the three of them had flown to Australia in advance of the wedding.

After dinner, the wine was still flowing and the conversation had turned to Geraint's job.

'Your boss is taking advantage of you,' my father announced, quickly adding, 'You have to ask for a raise,' effectively ordering Geraint.

My father held firm views about Geraint's employment. Over the past few days, he had relentlessly pressed Geraint to justify why he hadn't received a pay rise despite being their top salesman. It was an unfair situation, as Geraint was increasing sales for the company without receiving any recognition for his hard work. We could also do with the money, I was eager to repay our loans as soon as possible so we could sell the guesthouse and move on.

Geraint sulked in the corner, his cheeks flushed with anger and shame. I knew him well enough to understand that he didn't see my father's comments as helpful. To him, this was a personal attack, highlighting that he wasn't strong enough to manage his own affairs.

And the less Geraint said, the more my father talked.

I was squirming in my seat, not knowing what to do. On one side, I agreed with my father. Geraint did deserve a raise. And on the other hand, I was unsure how Geraint would react to his well-meant but direct words.

The result was quickly discovered when Geraint abruptly stood up, his chair scraping on the floor, and he stormed out of the room slamming the door behind him.

Stunned, my parents looked at each other, then at me.

'What just happened?' My father asked, surprise written on his face.

'I'll tell you what happened,' Sally snapped back, 'you're a bully and you've hurt my son.'

She was standing, hands clenched into fists and her hips aggressively thrust forwards.

'You've never liked him and you just can't stop yourself, can you? Keep your thoughts to yourself and leave my family alone.' Sally spat the last few words out, and before anyone had a chance to reply, she marched out, slamming the door behind her.

My parents and I sat in awkward silence as the events of the past few minutes sunk in.

'What on earth just happened?' my mother meekly repeated.

'I don't know, Mum. But I've got to find Geraint before it gets worse.'

Getting up, I could hear Geraint's car drive down our gravel driveway. I knew where he was heading.

Walking the 2.5km to the bottom of the road, I felt like I was in a twisted dream. The darkness enveloped me and whereas I would usually enjoy the feeling of the cool night air on my face, tonight it felt more like a sad omen for what was about to unfold.

As I predicted, Geraint's car was at the end of the road, with the door open and engine running, its main lights beaming out over the lookout ahead.

The road ended at a spectacular cliff, where the path fell vertically downwards for 400 metres. To the right, I could hear the waterfall splashing against the side of the cliff as it tumbled to the bottom of the valley.

Geraint was leaning on the barrier, his shoulders slumped as he stared out into the distance.

Approaching him from the side, I braced myself for what he was about to say. This wasn't the first time he had come to the cliff.

'Fuck your father. I fucking hate him. Who does he think he fucking is?' Geraint spat at me. 'Do you know what, if I kill myself, it'll be his fucking fault. He's so goddamn righteous and if I die, he'll then regret it. I fucking hate him.'

Silently listening to his words of hate, I let Geraint continue to talk.

I remembered the first time Geraint had come here. We'd had a disagreement about whether I should leave an unused fridge turned on, or turned off. I thought we could save energy and leave the fridge unplugged. Geraint thought otherwise.

We started to shout at each other, and he had stormed off, car keys in hand, 'Fuck you, Kate, you're so righteous and always get what you want. You have no idea how lucky you are that I put up with your shit.

Maybe you want me to kill myself too. Is that what you want?' he spat out at me.

He'd got into the car, and as I grasped at the passenger door, he pulled off, leaving me reeling at the thought that my boyfriend was about to drive off a cliff and that it was all my fault. Desperately, I ran to the end of the road, tears and snot running down my face.

I was trembling when I finally saw him gripping the barrier. 'I'm so sorry Geraint, I didn't mean it. We can leave the fridge on. Please, come back. I'm sorry.'

Tonight, Geraint's words were directed at my father, not me, and I could see that Geraint was hurting, but he was also emotionally manipulating people who he didn't agree with. His reaction was out of proportion to what was said. Looking at our future together, I knew he would never be there to support me, nor could I ever say 'no' to him again.

It was his way… or he'd threaten to kill himself.

I felt sorry for him. Geraint thought that this was the only way he could express a difference of opinion; the threat of death. We were toxic for each other and I had no idea why he wanted to live like this for the rest of his life.

Geraint ended his rant, exhausted from the release of such venomous emotions. We stood next to each other, not touching, looking out at the darkness.

Gently and numb from emotion, I said 'I can't marry you if you hate my family. You don't have to like them, but this outburst can't happen again.'

I let my words linger between us, the darkness of the night feeling a lot heavier than it did just moments ago.

In my heart, I knew Geraint would never back down from this outburst. He never apologised to me when he verbally attacked me, so the probability of him acting differently with my father was low.

Without turning, Geraint sighed deeply and said, 'Then I guess we're not getting married then.'

And as simple as that, it happened. I was shocked, not because we'd broken up, but because I felt nothing at all. not hollow, not sad, not relieved, nothing.

Nine years of life was over in a split second.

Slipping off my engagement ring, I unceremoniously placed it in a pocket of my jeans, making a mental note to return it to the real owner, my mother, later that evening.

For the next few days, I knew that I had to shelve any emotions and fears because I had close to 20 friends flying into Australia for a wedding that wasn't happening and I needed to show them I was okay.

And this is exactly what happened. Daily, friends dribbled in from the UK, Europe and Central America. I loved catching up with people I'd not seen for over a decade and after the initial shock of there being no groom, or wedding, we drank and celebrated coming together.

For four days, I don't recall having a sober moment. Alcohol was flowing morning, noon and night, and my feet barely touched the ground. Even on the 'non wedding day', I didn't have time to reflect on how I felt because we all went for a long walk in the surrounding Australian blue gum forest, followed by even more drinks.

Yet the day of everyone's departure arrived all too soon, and the reality that I was the only one who couldn't leave was the unspoken truth that hung between us.

'I'll miss you!' I shouted, running down the road after my friends, trying to hide that my heart was breaking behind this cliché joke.

It was true, I adored seeing them again and enjoyed us reminiscing of what we used to get up to in a life almost forgotten.

The last people to leave were my parents. They had tried to change their flights to be with me for longer, but it proved impossible and so their departure stayed the same, just two days after my non-wedding.

Standing in the foyer of my empty guesthouse, my mother couldn't hold back her tears and was sobbing behind a tissue. My father, struggling to console her, was nervously moving the bags side to side, a big frown casting a shadow over his eyes and biting on his lower lip so hard it had turned white.

I smiled, realising that, just like my Dad, I bit my lip when I struggled to process my emotions.

A car horn outside signalled the taxi's arrival and my mother burst into tears again, letting out a howl.

'Oh darling, I love you so much, I wish we could do more.'

My heart was breaking as I watched the pain she was in. My eyes started to water and my throat tightened. I didn't want to be alone and, all of a sudden, I felt like a little girl who wanted her mother and father to hug her and say it'll all be okay.

But I knew that they couldn't promise this. I had to step up and be as confident as I wished they could have been for me.

Clearing my throat, I awkwardly reached out and patted my mother's shoulder, 'I'll be fine, Mum, honest.' Smiling the biggest smile I could muster, I reached down and grabbed one of their bags.

'Come on, it's time to go,' I called out over my shoulder as I opened the front door and headed towards the taxi. I needed them to leave as soon as possible, or they would see me break down crying and heaving from the emptiness and dread I had about my present situation and bleak future.

Loading the bags, and my parents, in the taxi, there was barely time to hug, and before I knew it the taxi pulled off with two concerned faces peering from the back seat.

As I stood at the front gate waving my parent's taxi goodbye, it was the first real time in my life I felt completely alone.

Being selfish is the most selfless thing you can do

Being alone in the guesthouse was daunting. Even though I had been running the guesthouse single-handed for many years, I felt nervous and unsure that I was capable of managing the business alone. When Geraint left he also stopped contributing to our mortgage repayments, so what little money that was left over was absorbed in honouring our debt.

For the first few months I operated on auto pilot, waking up each morning to cook breakfast, make coffee, and check out guests. The afternoons were spent cleaning rooms and tending to the one-acre gardens attached to the property.

I had found myself engaged to a man who, even though at the beginning there was respect and probably even love, closer to our wedding date it was abundantly apparent that love had been slowly and gradually corroded, until what was left of me was a shell of a woman struggling to make a decision without permission from my partner.

Today, I can show compassion for my ex, realising that he had no means of communicating with somebody who may not have agreed with his point of view. But it still didn't excuse his controlling and manipulative behaviour that, in the past, would have left me on my knees hyperventilating through my tears, thinking that maybe what he was saying was right; that I was wicked and evil and somehow broken. Seeing his venomous attack directed towards someone else had broken the spell that he held over me. I knew that my father wasn't evil, even if his delivery was sometimes a little direct, he wanted to support and help both me and Geraint. I started to doubt I was such a bad person, and that maybe, just maybe, I deserved more than my current lot.

I was trying to find and build back the shattered pieces of my life and my self-esteem. But we only know how strong we are when we have to pass through these dark moments. Without such sadness and pressure, I may not have decided to work on myself.

During the mundane monotony of every day filled with the same cooking and cleaning tasks, I had time to reflect and explore my past. A pattern started to emerge as I reviewed the past nine years and beyond. I hadn't spoken up. The moments, at the beginning of our relationship, when he'd say, 'I miss you when you go to the gym,' and I'd reluctantly put away my sports bag, grabbing a wine glass to join him on the sofa, were pivotal moments where I compromised myself and my goals. I had helped create an environment where, at the end of our nine years, it was deemed acceptable to text me asking why I had left the house, or had spent $20 at the local grocery store? Throughout the latter years of our relationship, I found myself justifying every movement of my life. Due to the anxiety I felt when I went outside - fearing he would either call or text me asking why I had left the house, especially after he installed a tracker 'for security reasons' on my phone - I often decided to decline invitations to go out.

During our engagement, clawing at the final shreds of possibility for freedom, I decided to take up running, something I had enjoyed for nearly all of my life, and only stopped after meeting Geraint.

It doesn't take a psychologist to see that, as I couldn't escape my physical situation, I took up the sport that facilitated running away! Fearful of running also being taken from me, I used to hide my phone in our guesthouse's letterbox next to the front door. The phone was close to the lounge so, for Geraint's purposes, it looked like I was talking with guests or tending to the fire, but it afforded me the freedom to run in small circles, leaving my phone unattended for a justifiable 20 minutes. As my strength grew, I increased the number of loops, rather than running further along the road, to make sure I stayed within the safety zone of answering my phone within 20 minutes. I didn't want to lose the only thing I felt I had any sense of joy or control over within my life.

Finding myself single in 2013 was liberating but also terrifying at the same time. The box that I felt controlled and stuck within was finally removed. The external voice of my ex telling me I was a failure, that I always made the wrong decision, and reminding me of how many mistakes I had previously made, was replaced with my own inner dialogue, chastising myself for the simplest of tasks.

I covered up the mirrors in my living quarters because I couldn't bear to look at what I saw: A woman older than her age, carrying wrinkles, too thin in the wrong places and my body convex when it should have been concave. Nothing I saw in the mirror I liked.

I turned to alcohol to dull the edges. Initially, it was easier to drink away my problems than it was to actually confront them. Yet, gradually and over time, my evenings - and drinking - became more extreme. I enjoyed getting drunk, at that moment I could forget my problems and the reason I was drinking so much was all his fault.

I felt trapped in this business. Now single in my mid thirties, I couldn't help but think that my unhealthy state was partly his fault. Yet another extreme night out with my friends had ensued, with the parties becoming increasingly ridiculous. In an attempt to make the blur of these alcohol-fuelled evenings stand out, we found ourselves playing darks with a stick-on dildo, trying to hit a target we'd drawn on a glass window. Prancing around in shorts and a bra I'd fashioned out of two conical hats, we were singing and dancing to songs. Occasionally, we picked up a dildo, spun around, and threw it towards the window. I was already drunk, having started doing vodka shots at 3 in the afternoon.

In a rare moment of lucidity, I caught a glimpse of my reflection and paused. My future flashed in front of me. Would I be destined to endure more extreme evenings and more outlandish activities just to make each next night stand out from the last? How much more could I cope with, and how much more extreme did I need to become to convince myself, and the world, that I was fine?

My antics were attention-grabbing acts that screamed, 'I'm pretending that everything is good, but inside, I'm hurting.'

The reflection and subsequent 'ah ha' moment was a final cry for help from my inner self. I was still carrying resentment and toxicity against my ex that - until that moment - I refused to acknowledge or process. Tottering in high heels, gently swaying with a buzz from the last shot, I had a decision to make. Do I continue on this path of self-destruction, or do I start building my life back up?

I chose the latter.

I needed to do something for myself, something wholesome to build up my self-esteem, rather than distractions like dildo-darts. And with that thought, a memory from nearly a decade ago emerged. I recalled a woman who had inspired me to dream big while we sat on the side of a volcano at dawn.

To break this destructive pattern, I needed a goal that was entirely my own, almost selfish. Training for and competing in an Ironman seemed like a way to reclaim some of what I felt that I had lost. I can't remember if I said it out loud, but that night I declared, 'I'm going to do an Ironman.'

Maybe it was the alcohol, or maybe it was an actual moment of lucidity, but fuelled by the idea of reigniting a dream I thought that I had lost forever, I decided that I would no longer live beneath someone else's limited perception of me; I didn't just want to break glass ceilings; I wanted to live a life where they didn't even exist!

Applying this thought to my goal of becoming an Ironman, I realised that since I had never completed an Ironman triathlon before, I had no idea of my potential. Therefore, the only logical target to set for myself, without capping my ability, was to aim to win the competition. I was going to be a world champion!

The next day, after spending a long day making breakfasts and cleaning guest rooms while nursing a particularly painful hangover, I finally sat down. I could pretend that my decision the previous night hadn't happened, that I was fuelled by alcohol and made a mistake. Yet, something in me had shifted. No longer did I want to live a fearful and resentful life; instead, I wanted to stop wishing away my time and start exploring whether I could create more than fleeting moments of happiness for myself.

Still feeling a little delicate, I slowly walked to my office, which was a windowless and unheated box-room deep in the bowels of my guesthouse.I opened a new search browser and typed 'how do you win an Ironman triathlon?'

Through every spare minute during the following days, I devoured articles, watched videos, and read reports on what elements are needed to become a world champion. Deciding to focus on each aspect of the sport separately, I deconstructed what I would need to do that stretched far beyond just swimming, cycling and running. I read books on sleep patterns, bioavailability of food sources, change behaviour, and meditation. I sought out experts in each of these fields, with one question in mind: 'How will this help me win an Ironman?'

Gradually I felt that I had all the pieces of creating a world champion triathlete, and I now had the thrilling task of meticulously and deliberately designing who I needed to become. I was quite literally redesigning my thoughts, actions and behaviours to become a world champion triathlete from the ground up. Every single task that I thought a champion triathlete would be doing during their daily activities and their thought processes, I committed to mirroring and living exactly as per that formula.

I slowly started making the necessary changes. It wasn't easy, as I was still single-handedly working seven days a week in a hospitality business. As well as with the emotional pressure of still trying to untangle my life from my ex, who had recently started a lawsuit against me, I had many justified reasons to press <pause> on my idea of training to compete, let alone win an Ironman.

Yet, the triathlon represented so much more than potentially winning a gold medal. This was not a selfish act, this was me realigning my life and giving me purpose to heal and grow. Our lives, just like a bicycle wheel, only roll smoothly when the middle bit - the hub - is aligned properly. If we are able to correctly align our centre by putting ourselves first, not only can we roll faster and smoother through life, but we are also able to carry more with us, be that supporting friends or creating and implementing ideas to benefit others.

'Darling, I don't know why you do it.'

My ear was pressed to the phone as I quickly swallowed a mouthful of oats.

'Because I have no other option, Mum,' I replied, slightly muffled as I was part chewing and part swallowing my breakfast.

Still wearing my sweaty clothes, I had started to shiver in the cold bedroom. Turning the phone on speaker, I threw it on the bed as I kicked off my trainers and continued eating my breakfast.

'I know that, but running at 4am seems so extreme.'

Smiling, I silently shook my head. I loved my mother for caring so much. And regardless of what I said in response to her concerns, each week she would predictably say the same thing; in her opinion, I was doing too much.

Shovelling the last spoonful of muesli into my mouth, I hung up the phone, and headed to the shower. I had exactly five minutes to wash and dress before work started. My days were planned with precision and if I procrastinated, for even a few short minutes, it could mean the difference between reaching my goal… or not.

Ironman triathlon training was brutal. My training required me to swim for four and a half hours, cycle for sixteen hours and also squeeze in ten hours of running every single week. I had to find time for over thirty, THIRTY, hours of training, when I was already working seven days a week in the guesthouse. There was no time for excuses, procrastination or self-doubting. I needed to drop my whinging and lie-ins and honour my training.

And if this meant waking up before the sun rose and getting a few hours of cycling or running completed before I started work at

7:30am, then so be it. My alarm's snooze button was a distant memory and so was watching television. When my ex left me, he had also taken the TV, which ironically made it a little easier for me to focus on rest rather than late-night programmes! I was committed to squeezing out anything in my diary that wasn't directly helping me get fitter, more focused, or faster.

I was once told that in order to live a fulfilled life, there are only two questions we need to answer 'yes' to:

1. Do you love who you live with?

2. Do you love what you do for work?

For me, my answers were 'no,' and 'no.' Even though I loved the wilderness that surrounded me, my living situation challenged me. I had no choice but to live where I worked and that meant I was sleeping in an unheated corner of the guesthouse. Since my breakup with Geraint, I was quite literally tied to the property and financially forced to work every day to make sure there was enough money in the bank to pay suppliers and slowly repay our debt.

There were moments when, overly tired, cold and crying, I'd partly collapse, partly slump on the side of a road midway through yet another training set of 20 x 1km runs. I knew that I still had a lot of healing to do, and to rebuild my confidence, which had been corroded over the past nine years of mental, emotional and physical neglect, would take much longer than a few months of training.

Just eight months after I began training, I entered a long-distance triathlon to prepare for my Ironman a few months later. This race consisted of a 4 km (2.5 mile) swim, a 120 km (75 mile) cycle and a 30 km (19 mile) run. Surprisingly to everyone but me, I won my age group because, unlike them, I had been visualising every metre of the race before falling asleep. For months, I had visualised myself standing on the podium of a race, knowing that the hundreds of hours of training merited my reward. Yet, what was truly surprising was that this race automatically qualified me for the age-group team, securing me a place to compete in the World Championships in Weihai, China.

'Focus on the why, and the how will work itself out,' I repeated to myself once I had returned back to cleaning my guesthouse. I had no surplus money to afford the flights and accommodation, let alone the additional cost of hiring a replacement to work in the guesthouse. The logistics of me being able to compete far exceeded my resources and had I focused on the practical barriers of me being able to enter, I would have immediately given up. Instead, I continued to train, turning up every single day with the unwavering belief that I would get to the World Championships and a way to make this happen would unfold.

And unfold it did because, unbeknown to me, my daily pre-dawn runs and post-work cycles hadn't gone unnoticed. The sleepy village of 2,000 residents had been silently watching me as I ran up and down and up the roads, initially mocking me and my crazy dream. Yet their humour gradually turned into respect and later on pride. Thanks to my determination and, almost religious, commitment to do my best regardless of the weather, time of day, or temperature, they now were invested in me having an opportunity to realise my dream. A few months before the date of the World Championships, the village rallied around and raised enough money for my trip to China. If this weren't enough, they also organised some local hospitality students to manage my guesthouse while I was away.

My dream that initially started as a process for me to build up my confidence and give me permission to imagine a different future for myself was actually within my grasp.

Arriving in China was a huge shock to the system. Wei Hai was more humid than I could have ever imagined and whenever I left the cool air conditioning of my room I was surprised to be hit by a wall of heat and dampness that clung to my skin. Where I lived in Australia was 1,200m (3,900 feet) above sea level, so even on hot days, where temperatures exceed 35 degrees Celsius (95 Fahrenheit), rarely did I have to compete with the humidity. The air was cool and crisp to breathe, unlike the heavy air that was sticking to me in China.

I had arrived a few days earlier than most other competitors, wanting to take some time to switch off from my routine guesthouse chores and switch on time to rest and recharge. One morning, as I was meandering back from breakfast, contemplating if I would take a cat-nap or write in my journal for a bit, I caught a glimpse of a bike travel bag in the foyer. Slowing down, I looked over, trying to see if the person checking in was a man, or woman - would they be a fellow competitor, I mused. The person at the reception was definitely a female triathlete. She was shorter than me, with long brown hair loosely held in a braid. Wearing bright yellow and green clothes, initially I thought she was another Australian athlete, but quickly heard her thick Latin American accent confidently requesting help with her bags. 'No, I can't carry these bags, they are too heavy for me. I am Brazil number one, I need my key and rest. You bring them up later, okay?'

I didn't know if what she said was a question or a statement, but either way, 'MIOTTO', the name written on her bags and clothes, walked off in the direction of the rooms. Until this moment, I had not seen a 'competitor' in China. Until now, I had always raced for myself - to be my best and to beat my own personal demons. Yet, here was a true competitor and potential obstacle to me achieving my goal of being world champion.

I didn't know the etiquette for athletes who are in the same race, so I decided to put the potential of us being competitors to the side and to just be me. Walking a little faster, I caught up with her.

'Hi, did you get in today?' Slightly startled, she turned to face me.

'Yes. Paula. Pleased to meet you,' she said, reaching her hand out to shake mine.

'Kate. Likewise,' I replied smiling, grateful that she seemed friendly and eager to connect.

'Which country are you competing for?' she asked, quickly scanning my clothes for clues.

'Australia, but I was born in Wales.'

A smile broke across her face, 'Ah, Australia. I love the beaches there! We are going to be friends, but first, I need to rest. See you at dinner.'

Turning on her heel, she carried on walking towards her room, assuming that I agreed with her invitation/order.

Smiling, I opened my door, happy that I had made one new friend.

Race day arrived quickly, and standing on the beach feeling the coarse sand between my toes I looked around at the other competitors. I was in the fifth group to start, with the professional athletes having started their race one hour before us.

It was a late start for a triathlon and the sun was steadily climbing in the sky, adding degrees of heat and uncomfortableness as I stood shuffling and sweating in my wetsuit.

Looking around, I tried to avoid eye contact with the others and realised this was a relatively simple task to achieve. Most women were in their own bubble of focus.

'They look so fit and confident, better than you could ever be,' my inner voice said to myself as a few girls practised running and diving into the water. As soon as I heard this voice starting to criticise me and add doubt to who I was, I immediately shut it down with love, 'Kate, you have done your best. You've given it your 100%. Race for the joy of racing and with your heart full of pride and for being able to be here today!'

I wasn't here to beat anyone. I wanted to do my best, and could be happy with whatever the result was. Looking back over the past 14 months, there was not a moment I would change. I had stepped over my own insecurities, ignored the hatred my ex had thrown at me, and overcome the many reasons that should've prevented me from making the starting line. I had chosen the hard path of training, discipline, and routine. Today was my reward. Today I earned the right to compete for Australia and be proud of who I was becoming: A woman with a place in this world!

Today's race is my reward for my hard work, not the result at the end. Regardless if I came first or last, I knew that I was the best I had ever been in my life. This moment was all I needed.

Tears started to well in my eyes and, as I pulled my goggles off to rub the fog off the lenses, 'bang,' the starting gun sounded and hundreds of women lurched forward towards the water's edge.

Quickly pushing my goggles back on, I started running down the beach and towards the splash of women already entering the water. I don't like beach start races, preferring to already be in the water gently floating and waiting for the start. As the water got deeper, I didn't know when it was time to dive into the water and start swimming. Looking across, I could see most women were diving in and, using their hands to push off from the bottom, catapulting their bodies out of the water and further along. I didn't want to try that and risk losing my goggles, or accidentally swallowing the polluted water, so I continued running, raising my knees high above the water, until it was too deep to continue.

The night before, some athletes had shared a report stating that the water quality had greater than 2.2ppM faecal matter, a 'high-risk level' as per the government site. Disgusted at the thought of swimming through raw sewage, I decided to keep my mouth closed in the water, even if this meant swimming slower.

Wading in just below my waist, I took a deep breath, closed my mouth, and dove in. Feeling the cool water slap my face calmed me down, and the noise and splashing of the other athletes was muffled. Getting into my steady rhythm of front crawl, I swam outwards, away from the shore and towards the turning point about 1 km (0.62 miles) in the distance.

It always surprises me that when I am swimming in a race, however manic and tightly cramped I feel at the starting line, I find space and solitude so quickly in the water, and today was no exception. Within a few strokes I was relatively alone, with the exception of one swimmer about 1 metre (3 feet) to my side.

The swim comprised two laps of a 2 km (1.24 miles) 'square' marked out in the bay where, after completing one lap, I'd need to exit the water, run a short distance across the beach to re-enter the water and continue swimming.

Once I had completed the 4 km (2.5 miles) swim, there was a 2-loop bike course totalling 120 km (74.5 miles) and a four-loop run route that had been shortened from 30 km (18.6 miles) to 20 km (12.4 miles). That morning, when the officials had announced that the run would be shortened by a third due to the high humidity, I was gutted. Running was where I shone and I could potentially catch up to some stronger cyclists. Having a shorter run-distance meant I needed to be faster on the bike, which might not be a possibility.

Back in the water, I felt strong as my fingers glided through the water. I saw no need to sprint in the swim, as there were many hours and miles between me and the finish line. Now was a time to get into the 'zone', to feel completely present and at one with my body and mind. I used the swim to wash away any negative thoughts and insecurities about my fitness and potential in possibly winning the race.

Feeling my fingers dig into the sand, I knew I was close to completing the swim. Jumping up, I pulled my goggles off before they fogged over and ran towards the beach. I could hear the roar of the spectators and locals with screams and shouts mixed in with a tribal drumming in the distance.

The bike ride was a joy of taking in the dramatic coastline of China, along with a heart-pounding band rhythmically drumming to motivate us up one of the hills along our route. I had pre-determined the speed I would cycle at, and even though I wanted to go faster, I knew that if I pushed, even a little bit harder than planned, I might cycle two minutes quicker, yet risk running fifteen or more minutes slower. 'Trust the plan,' I repeated each time I felt the urge to catch up to a cyclist drifting just ahead of me, or felt surged on by the crowds cheering.

Time passed swiftly, and the end of my second loop was drawing close to the increasing sounds and screams of spectators waving their country flags and banners supporting the competitors. Running into the transition zone, I noticed that there were other bikes already in place, signalling that I had at least six women ahead of me. Throwing my helmet into my bag while effortlessly pulling on my trainers, I left the transition area in under two minutes.

Rolling my shoulders back, slowing my breathing and shortening my running gait to give my legs time to adjust from the restricted position of cycling to the free-flowing rotation of running, I blew a kiss to my parents and ran.

Now wasn't the time to hold back, nor run within my pre-conceived capabilities, so I decided to twist my watch to face the road and out of eyeshot. Typically I use my watch to govern my pace, to not run too slow nor too fast - keeping me in my 'sweet spot' of performance. Today, if I wanted a chance to win, I needed to unleash myself and run like I never had run before, I needed to run like a world champion.

You're at the top, so what?

'I can't believe it! What does it mean?'

My mother kept repeating these words, and only until I held her in my arms, cradling her head, feeling her trembling hands wrapped around my waist did she finally absorb that her daughter was number one in the world for her age-group. I had lived through pain, through maliciousness, and instead of being bitter and twisted from the experience, I'd shifted what could have easily been hate into a force that drove me to be my best. And today I had delivered my best, and my best was World Champion!

To be slightly pedantic, I was the age-group world champion, not the overall world champion. Also I was age-group world champion for long-distance, and not Ironman distance triathlon as per my original goal, but it didn't detract from the elation and joy I felt exuding from my heart.

Over the subsequent years, try as I might, I never achieved more than 10th position in Ironman Asia Pacific Championships, and my dream of being an Ironman world champion was kept out of reach. Yet, I had found my personal best and had done so without capping my potential to anything less than what I was capable of. Thanks to not having put a glass ceiling on my potential, I was satisfied that I had reached my full capacity in triathlon.

Within a few months of me leaving China with my gold medal (which was actually a plastic medal sprayed gold) and returning to my daily routine of cleaning rooms and cooking breakfasts, I was also finally able to settle the legal dispute with my ex and sell the guesthouse, freeing myself from the seven day a week 'groundhog day' experience that I'd been living for the past few years.

My time in Australia felt like it had run its course and it was time to move back to Britain. I was ready for a change of scenery. It was during this time that I realised that emotionally, I was struggling. I might have been at the top of my physical game, but I had given no time for fully healing the trauma that I had been running away from through my triathlon.

Moving back into my childhood bedroom, I decided to take up yoga to remove the pressure of performance and, hopefully, unwind the nervous energy and insatiable desire to be doing something all the time. Yet, in my second class, while kneeling, I lent back to the unfamiliar position of touching my toes from over my head and I felt a shooting pain in my right hip with my right leg being catapulted forward, leaving me acutely aware that something was wrong.

After days of experiencing a pain so intense that I struggled to walk let alone run, a CT scan confirmed that I had torn a ligament in my hip and, probably, would never be able to run again if I didn't undergo an operation. Even if I had the operation, I definitely would never run anything further than a half marathon. My running, and triathlon, days were over, along with my identity of being a triathlete.

Sport has consistently helped me reclaim my courage and confidence. It has been my councillor and confidant through my time of distress, giving me space to process what I'm feeling without being judged. It also offers me a place to celebrate failing, where I might otherwise see it as something to avoid. Athletes train until we fail. We set the run targets just ahead of what's comfortable, or lift weights where the final rep is almost impossible. We intuitively understand that we need to be okay with not meeting our targets in training sessions, enabling us to improve. What I love most about sport is that every single lesson learnt - embracing failure as part of the journey, allowing raw emotions to emerge, and the discipline required to create and commit to a plan - translates so well to other areas of our lives.

For that reason, a few years after moving back to the UK I felt it was time to seek out a new sporting goal. My personal and professional life had plateaued, and I was ready to 'uplevel', by using sport as my mentor to support this transformation. Not wanting to compete against others, and still not being able to run without pain, I wanted to step away from triathlon and competitive events.

In competitions, even if I trained my hardest and had a perfect race day, my performance was still compared to others' and the result might not reflect my effort. I no longer wanted my performance to be based on other people's performance, nor for my current results to be compared to my past performances either.

I also wanted to use sport for something greater than for my personal healing. I toyed with what sport represented to me. It had not only helped me grow and hold me accountable to stepping into a bigger version of myself, but it also represented a means of positive advocacy. One night, while passing the time by aimlessly scrolling through the Guinness World Records website, I noticed that there was a disproportionate amount of sporting World Records for men compared to the equivalent records for women. One particular record caught my eye: The furthest distance on a static bike in 24 hours. There was a male world record but no female equivalent.

'Maybe, just maybe, I could attempt this record,' I mused. The attempt would prove beneficial for my personal growth through building up my confidence and keeping my competitive spirit alive. And, unlike triathlon, I would only be competing against myself rather than others.

In addition to the record being a part of my personal healing journey, I could also use this record attempt as a means to talk about the importance of fair gender representation in sport. That evening, my path was decided and I applied to attempt the record a mere six months later under the misguided assumption that I was physically and mentally ready for the attempt and that, seeing that it was a world's first attempt, any distance I cycled, however small, would earn me a world record.

My first attempt in 2017 was a failure. As predicted, I had not trained effectively or enough, being more focused on the hope that just because it was a world first attempt would mean that I could be given the world record. Even though I cycled for 24 hours and covered close to 300 miles (777 km), Guinness rejected my application on the premise that the distance wasn't far enough.

At the time, my pride and my body shut down any idea of reattempting the record. I was hurting both physically and emotionally and carrying a layer of shame and guilt - shame for not applying the discipline the world record demanded, and shame for letting down many friends who had come to support me throughout the 24 hours.

I knew that I had never fully committed to a training plan, and had arrogantly assumed that records were easy to achieve. It took me three years to acknowledge that this half-assed attempt would forever haunt me unless I reattempted it and properly trained for the record. I had not been my best version of myself, and I knew that I deserved to discover if I was actually capable of earning a world record.

And as the world slowly closed down during the 2020 lockdown, earlier that year, I had already bought an indoor bike trainer and had started cycling just 30 minutes, three times a week, with the intention to slowly increase my training, peaking at the end of the year for an official - and fully committed - attempt.

The first date for my record was postponed due to lockdown regulations tightening.

'No worries,' I said to myself, 'it gives me more time to train,' rationalising the additional few months I had to sustain peak mental and physical performance.

With just two days before my second date, another nation-wide lockdown was announced and this time, there was no end in sight for how long we would be forced to stay indoors.

To complete my world record, I had coerced over twenty friends to support me through the 24 hours. Not only would I need help in feeding me and changing the towel I would be sitting on that would absorb my pee - allowing me to keep cycling rather than waste precious time to visit the bathroom, I also needed witnesses to officiate the record.

I immediately organised a group call with my friends to discuss options. Evident that we would be breaking social distancing rules if we continued with the world record, I coughed away any sign of tears that were bubbling underneath the surface. At this point, I had been training for thirteen months and built my training to perfectly peak at the date for the world record. For months, I had been cycling in the corner of a bedroom for upwards of eight hours a day, with little distraction but the occasional car driving past the window of the flat. My (now ex) partner - who I had moved in with during lockdown - had put up with many date nights involving him sitting on the sofa, enjoying a pizza while I cycled next to him, turning the TV volume to maximum to cut out the drone of my bike turbo trainer.

I refused to let my world record day slip away unnoticed. I wanted to - needed to - celebrate the commitment delivered by me and also my crew.

'Let's go ahead, with changes' I announced, realising that I needed some peak to grasp towards, even if it wasn't the one I had originally trained for.

So, on the coldest day of the year, instead of cycling for 24 hours, I cycled for one hour. And, instead of twenty friends supporting and cheering me on, two neighbours watched my record attempt through their lounge windows. My friends joined me virtually while, for sixty minutes, I heaved and groaned, struggling to take in oxygen as the bitterly cold air pierced my lungs. I despise short and fast distances, so was fully expecting my effort to fall short of the already existing world record of 23.1 miles (37.17 km), yet just as I collapsed, heaving and coughing on my handlebars, I could hear the screaming from my friends 'you've done it!'

With one world record achieved, it gave me fuel to keep training and develop the skill of patience, something I'm not typically known for! I didn't know when I could attempt the 24-hour record, and there was nothing I could do that would accelerate lockdown being lifted, freeing me to sit on a bike for 24 hours.

Eventually, I was able to set a date for my attempt, and I chose the evening of a full moon in May. For the record, I had exhibited discipline and tried to control as many elements as possible. Yet, I was constantly reminded that there were elements beyond my grasp that could impact the best laid plans. The minute I started pedalling, I had to surrender to whatever may happen. My bike was positioned outside Clifton Observatory in Bristol, overlooking the famous suspension bridge. I was at the mercy of the elements, yet I was also drawing in energy from the natural surroundings. As dusk fell on us, my rhythmical click of the rotations of my pedals blended into the evening ticking bugs, calling out to each other under the rising full moon.

As the dawn chorus of birds alerted us to the imminent sunrise, their song briefly distracted me from my physical pain. It overshadowed my groans as I accidentally caught another open wound while desperately trying to adjust my seating position. I sought in vain for any position that could relieve the pain of cycling on open wounds, areas split open from many hours of chafing.

The original plan was for my crew to advise me each hour whether I was on or off track from the total distance target. However, as the hours dragged on, my ability to focus diminished significantly, and targets were adjusted to every few minutes.

'Can you cycle for ten more minutes?' Shameek tentatively asked. I didn't need to say a word because my eyes cut through the question with a resounding 'absolutely not.'

'Okay, okay,' he said, raising his hands in defence, 'we'll go for five minutes.'

And, that's how I cycled for twenty-four hours, dangling the carrot of a possible break every five minutes. Then, at 3pm on 26 May 2021, I set a new world record for the greatest virtual distance on a static cycle in 24 hours, covering 433.09 miles (565.67 km)! As a 'fun' bonus, I also broke the 1- and 12-hour records along the way.

The evolution of my sport had grown from competition with others to competition with myself, and I was excited about the potential that my world record attempt had opened the possibility for other women and individuals to be inspired to dream big and stretch towards a bold goal.

Alas, this hope of inspiring the masses didn't happen exactly as I had dreamed of. Even though people could witness first-hand me crying through the pain of yet another part of my body bleeding from chafing or over-use, they felt disconnected to what I was attempting from what they thought was possible for them, with most people saying 'you're amazing, but I could never do that.'

It didn't matter that only two years ago, I was cycling for just 30 minutes. It was only through consistency that I grew in strength to entertain cycling for this long. I saw - and still do see - myself as an ordinary woman. Yet, what is unconventional is that I am prepared to attempt the extraordinary and push through the barriers of my comfort zone, as well as limiting beliefs, surrounding my own potential.

Even though I had found a way to compete against myself, rather than others, I was in my mid-40s and really didn't want to keep beating my body up to make a point. It's fatiguing, tiring and, honestly, I was aching and creaking from the strain of what I'd done!

There had to be a better way to use sport as a vehicle to connect people with causes and also, possibly even more important, enable them to be part of the journey rather than as observers to what I was doing.

At the same time that lockdown was lifted, so too did my ignorance around the current fragile state of our planet. I had always been aware of the issues of global warming and climate change, just as I was aware of wars in distant lands, but they seemed far away from me in location as well as in timeline: This wasn't a 'today' or 'here' concern.

Yet, as human activity picked up its pace with the lifting of lockdown rules and people returned to 'normal' practices, I noticed a change in my own suburb. The bird song once filled my daily walks was now muffled with the drone of cars on a new bypass. The quiet walks through flowering meadows were becoming waterlogged and muddy due to increased rainfall and nearby fields being built upon. Nature was struggling, and so were we.

Why now?

You don't need to lift your head up too far from our daily routine to stumble across an aspect of the world that requires support and remodelling. Our mental health is at an all-time low, with more people on antidepressants and struggling with isolation and depression than ever before. Physically we're not doing too well either, with the annual cost for diabetes for the NHS being £25,000 every minute. That's a whopping £14 billion pounds each year[1]. With 90% of people living with diabetes are Type II diabetes, which is largely reversible with lifestyle and dietary changes[2], it seems illogical that we're spending more on treating a debilitating illness than preventing it in the first place.

Socially we are also crumbling. What I sadly call 'the othering' is creating divides, keeping us separate from our communities and disconnected from friends with differing viewpoints. The vast list of problems we face extends far beyond this limited list, and I believe they could be resolved quicker, with less struggle and suffering, if we communicated and worked together. Yet we're encouraged to fear those we don't know and judge those that don't share our opinions.

---

[1] https://www.diabetes.co.uk/cost-of-diabetes.html
[2] https://www.webmd.com/diabetes/can-you-reverse-type-2-diabetes

I noticed myself sitting within an ever decreasing circle of friends who mostly agreed with my viewpoints. Even though it was - and still is - fun to hang out with my small clan of nomadic plant-based athletes, there was very little space for me to grow and be challenged on whether my views were still serving me or even valid.

I know that our comfort zone is no place for growth and expansion, and I sensed that I needed a big personal challenge, something way past what I had ever done before to pull me out of this cosy groove of being right. I find that when I devise a huge physical challenge, something so big I actually feel scared thinking about how to start developing it, other aspects of my life start stepping up to the level of the new challenge. We can't uplevel in one area of our life without the other areas being forced to uplevel too.

Originally, I toyed with entering the self-proclaimed world's toughest road race, the Race Across America (RAAM). However, flying ten people to the States to cycle rapidly through some sacred First Nations land didn't sit well with me on many levels. Returning to the drawing board, I kept the distance of RAAM, 3,000 miles (4,828 km), as at least one focal point to build upon.

I deconstructed the concept of RAAM into a detailed list of components and opinions and I explored every line, asking myself, if I don't like [cycling fast], what do I like?'

Over many weeks, the Climate Cycle was born. I would cycle 3,000 miles (4,828 km) around Britain (no flying) by myself and unaided (no vehicles required). Taking three months (slow cycling), I would also visit 30 community-led projects (pause to connect).

I also wanted to use the Climate Cycle as a means to meet people different from myself and see how they live, what their motivations are and what's important to them, while also challenging my own views and beliefs.

Could I rely on the generosity of strangers to help me throughout my cycle while also having conversations with people who, at first glance, had opposing views from myself?

Nearly every decision I made, from the food I would eat to the clothes I'd wear, I made with conscious deliberation. I have a slightly obsessive personality, and when a topic piques my interest I typically spend many hours researching and reading about it. My preferred places to read are peer-reviewed science journals, doing my best to avoid sponsored or biassed articles that are pushing a hidden agenda.

From this perspective, during my triathlon era, I stopped eating dairy, followed quickly by meat and eggs. The data linking these foods to diseases such as asthma, psoriasis, and even some cancers was enough for me to stop consuming them over 10 years ago[3].

It didn't take long for me to realise that living a plant-based lifestyle not only benefited my personal health but also had significant environmental advantages. The land requirements for a plant-based diet are four times less than those for a meat-dominant diet[4]. Additionally, in the face of an increasing water shortages, vegetables require significantly less water to produce[5], and this doesn't even take into account the increased greenhouse gas emissions generated from animal agriculture.

Today I don't have children, I don't buy leather and avoid 'virgin' cotton, I don't own a car, opting to travel either by bike, public transport or sharing a lift with friends, I also don't own or rent a house. If I buy clothes, they are typically second-hand from e-bay or charity shops, and I own a sewing machine, preferring to repair my clothes and shoes rather than throwing them away.

---

[3] https://www.pcrm.org/good-nutrition/nutrition-information/health-concerns-about-dairy
[4] https://ourworldindata.org/land-use-diets
[5] https://foodprint.org/issues/the-water-footprint-of-food/

I know that I'm living quite an extreme lifestyle. The Climate Cycle gave me a framework to explore if my decisions are actually 'moving the dial' when it comes to mitigating climate change, or was I wasting valuable space in my brain and time over small details, when I could be doing something completely different and much more impactful?

The Climate Cycle would, hopefully, give me the space to explore my decisions, and also expose me to opposing viewpoints and alternative activism actions that could help me decide anew what I could - and should - be doing.

More than a bike ride

I believe that most people who take up extreme sports or embark on enormous adventures have experienced some level of pain, trauma or 'darkness' in their lives that motivated them to do what they do. I am no exception. The Climate Cycle served as a vital part of my own personal healing journey from a toxic relationship that entrapped me for nine years and the subsequent decade, unbeknownst to me, I found myself repeating old patterns of victimhood, inadvertently attracting individuals to play the role of persecutor, thus perpetuating my my traumatised 'comfort zone'.

The Climate Cycle, ironically, was not about the bike, it was about the people. The bike ride was just the piece of string connecting the stories together.

Every single metre of the route was visible, giving members of the public the opportunity to join me. It was important the cycle wasn't 'just' me, but involved as many people as possible, be that the communities I stopped to visit or people jumping on their bike to cycle with me as I passed through their village or town. 'Join me for an hour, a day or a week,' I said regularly in the interviews leading up to the start of the cycle. And this is exactly what happened: throughout my 90 days on the road, 105 people cycled with me.

I also launched a virtual cycle through an app called Climategames for people who wanted to take part but couldn't meet me in person. Additionally, I created a private WhatsApp group for people to join and feel connected to me, the projects I was visiting, and the cycle route. Even on days when I was particularly exhausted from an intense day of cycling and cursed the extra admin I had to complete to keep the route up-to-date, I was so grateful for people making time to join me, even if only for an hour. These moments of companionship lifted my spirits far beyond anything imaginable.

Each community and project I visited was taking affirmative action to mitigate climate change. My mission was to seek out the success stories and positive examples where declining numbers were being reversed or toxins were being replaced by natural alternatives. I know that I'm not alone in feeling resigned and overwhelmed by the media's focus on seemingly negative news about the dire future of our country - and humanity. In fact, 46% of Brits avoid the news due to it bringing them down[6].

We do need to know the truth because staying in an overly optimistic bubble of hope and ignorance won't elicit the necessary changes we all need to start healing our planet. Regarding the climate crisis, there is a fine balance between being overly optimistic, sharing the harsh truth that creates the overwhelming sense of doom, and deflecting focus away from the subject entirely. Personally, I feel that the UK media has much to improve and is avoiding addressing the root issues we currently face.

---

[6] https://reutersinstitute.politics.ox.ac.uk/digital-news-report/2022#:~:text=46%25%20say%20they%20avoid%20the,the%20level%20seen%20in%202016

The goal of the Climate Cycle was to nurture the belief that we can make a meaningful impact on the immense changes required and to connect us with stories we can tangibly and realistically get involved in.

Drawing a rough circle around the coastline of Britain on a map I had pinned to my bedroom wall, I decided that this would be my official route. Now, all I had to do was find 30 different projects to visit and explore. I didn't want to repeat any project theme more than once, so if I completed a beach cleanup in Scarborough then I couldn't clean a second beach in Southampton. I wanted to see the various actions and solutions that people had created, and diversity was the key.

One of my personality traits that I love - and loathe - is my naivety. I adore that I have a child-like belief that anything is possible, and that it'll be simple. I get over-excited about things, and my imagination spirals upwards into ever increasing circles of grandeur. My imagination runs wild with what else could happen and, just like dominoes lined up in a row, once I start imagining one thing happening, another idea then another and another keeps getting added to the list.

Yet this naivety often catches me out, as I tend to agree to projects without fully assessing their enormity, leaving me with much more work to complete than I initially thought.

The Climate Cycle was no different. As my mind wandered in wonderful ways, so, too did the project expand into something much more than 'just' a cycle visiting some projects.

>What if my bike was made of natural materials, like bamboo?

>What if I only ate foraged foods?

>What if I could also track my air quality as I cycled?

What if I could speak at every school along the route?

What if I could plant 3,000 trees, one for each mile cycled?

Bigger and bigger, my imagination grew and for each new idea. I wrote it on a post-it note and stuck it onto the map. The route I had initially drawn was barely visible for all the little notes and ideas covering it.

Taking a step back from the map, I gazed at it lovingly, with the pride of a mother receiving a pasta birthday card from her daughter. It was ugly and made little sense, but it was made with passion and was one of the most beautiful things I had seen, even though its use was questionable.

My naive self loved the crazy, haphazard map. Yet, realising that I now had to deliver upon each sticky note and idea, the realisation that this project was way more complicated than first thought hit home.

How could I find each of these projects?

What is the probability that the projects would be equally distant between each other and conveniently located along my route around Britain?

The projects were vast and hugely different, with little cohesion between them. They ranged from refugee centres making apple juice, to seaweed farms, as well as temporary accommodation for the homeless to fermented shampoo bars! Even me - the creator of the project - was confused about what on earth I was visiting, and why. I needed to go back to the drawing board and create a simple story to link the projects to the Climate Cycle and the people joining me.

Yet, I'm getting ahead of myself: there's a few assumptions I'd like to address, starting with the climate crisis and the question: what, exactly, is sustainability?

What is sustainability?

The topics of the climate crisis and sustainability are vast with exploration possible from many different angles, ranging from poverty and gender inequality to water pollution and biodiversity loss. Back in 1997, the first degree I completed was in Environmental Engineering. Throughout my four years of study, I don't ever recall hearing the word 'sustainability' being uttered. Our focus was more on the treatment of waste, mostly in the water and on the land. Sustainability is a relatively new, trendy word thrown around to assure us of the neutral impact on the world. By purchasing from 'sustainable companies', we are led to believe we aren't causing harm.

The best description I've read for sustainability is from 1978 Brundtland Commission report for the United Nations[7]:

Sustainability means meeting our own needs without compromising the ability of future generations to meet their own needs.

---

[7] https://www.un.org/en/academic-impact/sustainability

I love this definition because it conjures up an image of a flowing river, where the river represents my family lineage. The source and the first ripples of the river represent my ancestors. The river stretching downstream from me represents the generations to come. I was 'born' on the bank of the river with whatever resources my ancestors created - whether that be a clear, flowing, healthy source of water, or a weakened and possibly polluted river. Of course, this is a hugely simplified metaphor because there are external variables that impact personal situations far beyond our control. Yet, in its simple concept, I like it: I live with the lot I was given and can still be responsible, ensuring that I don't impact the people downstream from me.

Yet, we do need something more tangible to effectively assess whether our actions and interactions are positively, or negatively impacting those downstream of us.

Sustainability is an enduring balanced approach to economic activity, environmental responsibility and social progress[8].

Simply put, sustainability encompasses three core elements:

- People
- Planet
- Prosperity

Picture a dart board, featuring three circles nested within one another. At its centre lies a small circle enclosed by a medium-sized one, which, in turn, is encompassed by the third and final circle.

The smallest circle in the middle represents **prosperity**: Unless we are economically stable and in a position to support ourselves, whether discussing individuals, companies or institutions, we cannot survive.

---

[8] https://www.iso.org/obp/ui/#iso:std:iso:20121:ed-1:v1:en:term:3.1

The second, middle circle represents **people**: Once our basic needs are looked after, we can now expand our attention to others. This might start off with people directly in our lives, such as family, co-workers and neighbours. Yet, this could expand over time to communities further afield.

The final and largest circle is the **planet**: Knowing that ourselves, our family and society are supported, we can now expand our reach to non-human sentient beings and the natural world that is so important for our survival.

Most governments, companies, family units, and individuals might start off with the best of intentions to consider the entire circle, yet many of us fall short of expanding past the first and a small second circle. We fall victim to being busy and slowly stop looking past our modest circle of 'care'. Life fills up, we work longer hours, and the fear of not having enough for us slowly pushes any non-urgent tasks down the priority list until, one day, they're no longer on the list at all.

We don't protect what we don't like, and we don't like what we don't know. So, how can we be expected to care about one of the fastest-declining bird species, the lesser spotted woodpecker[9], or the 900,000 school-age children who can't afford a school lunch[10], when we barely have the time or energy to tend to our own garden and families?

We are so busy commuting long hours to work, earning money to pay rent (or a mortgage) in an area that, by the end of the long working week, we barely have time to enjoy and explore. There's little surprise that we - as a society - have gradually been disconnecting from the mostly forgotten knowledge that we are all connected, and

---

[9] https://www.wildlifetrusts.org/wildlife-explorer/birds/woodpeckers-cuckoo-kingfisher-and-waxwing/lesser-spotted-woodpecker
[10] https://cpag.org.uk/sites/default/files/2023-08/Free%20school%20meals-%20third%20of%20kids%20in%20poverty%20miss%20out.pdf

sit within nature, rather than outside it. For us to truly thrive and be prosperous then we need to return to the natural rhythms that make us human, breaking away from the robotic and unnatural 9-5 routine and being chained to sell part of our life for money that might buy-back a sliver of happiness in our pre-approved annual holiday.

If we could reclaim a moment to simply be, freeing ourselves from the addiction to constantly do something, even if just for a moment, we might realise that we are only as 'happy' or as 'well off' as the lowest layer of who and what surrounds us. If insects are dying, so are we. If people are suffering, so are we.

For a whistle-stop bike ride around Britain, discussing the moral and philosophical implications of the intrinsic corruption of society seemed a little too big to address, even for me. So, I simplified things by choosing five themes that I felt had the greatest impact of our daily lives. Each project visited would represent at least one of these themes:

1. **Food**: What we eat and where we source our food
2. **Home and Energy**: How we live
3. **Travel**: Where we travel to (especially holidays), and how we get there
4. **Nature**: Ways we interact with and enjoy natural habitats
5. **Fun**: Things that we can enjoy today while also helping reduce our impact

Food

What we eat and how it's produced accounts for about a third of all human-caused greenhouse gas emissions, with the largest chunk of this footprint coming from agriculture and land use[11].

I was keen to discover methods to reduce food waste, and also explore how we can have a smaller footprint in the production of our food.

Being passionately plant-based, my ego wanted to find projects to prove me right around not eating meat or dairy, and to exclusively visit plant-based farms and other locations. Yet the project needed a greater diversity of voices within this theme.

I had to let go of my desire to be proven right, and I actively sought out smallholdings who ate spinach and sheep grown on their land, as well as bug farms, who raised insects to eat.

I also wanted to use these projects to revisit my personal beliefs and choices and make sure that I hadn't become stuck with actions that served an outdated philosophy.

Home and energy

Our energy requirements are only set to increase, thanks to the increasing use of electric cars and bikes, as well as the multiple electrical devices we all need to remain 'connected' by interacting online with our friends rather than playing frisbee in a field.

I wanted to explore the impact of us using more energy for wider land use, and also explore possible ways communities could work

---

[11] https://www.un.org/en/climatechange/science/climate-issues/food

together, generating energy from renewable sources rather than be dependent on the grid and foreign oil and gas?

I did not have time to visit any projects about home design, though being the daughter of a quantity surveyor and having spent many childhood hours visiting housing estates while my Dad worked over the weekend, I am interested in exploring the initial house design and seeing how even economical new-build houses could be more environmentally friendly, as well as reduce household bills. Maybe that'll be my next adventure…?

Travel

The more we travel, the more emissions we produce. Flying is one of the largest emission-generators in the travel sector, so is there a way for me, an ex heavy-flyer and exotic-location seeker, to fall in love with Britain and start seeing being 'trapped' on an island as an opportunity to explore more locally?

Another curious stat about travelling is 59% of most car trips are for 5 miles or less[12].

Could we pivot our dependence away from emission-polluters (including electric cars because their tyres and components will need to be replaced sooner) to a greener mode of travel, especially for these shorter trips?

---

[12] https://www.gov.uk/government/statistics/national-travel-survey-2020/national-travel-survey-2020

Nature-based solutions

It's all fair and well reducing our environmental impact and carbon footprint, yet we also need to ensure that these habitats are also restored, repaired and protected.

Since the Industrial Revolution, Britain has lost over 57% of its biodiversity, and is ranked in the bottom 10% globally for nature-depleted nations[13].

For us Brits, I think one of the issues we face is that we don't immediately see the loss around us, something I now know is called Shifting Baseline Syndrome: Over a prolonged period of time, we are unable to see what is being lost in front of us and get used to a different level of acceptability.

I like to use my mobile phone's battery as an example. When I first got my mobile (I did buy a second hand reconditioned iPhone in case you're curious), I needed to charge it every other day. My phone could comfortably stay switched on and in use for 48 hours. Yet, gradually and over time, I had to give it a little boost in the middle of the second day, then every evening. Today, I have to carry an external charger with me because it barely lasts an afternoon (to be fair, I did drop my beloved phone quite a few times while cycling around Britain, which definitely didn't help matters).

Had the change from needing to charge my phone every other day to running low on battery twice a day had happened overnight, I would have predictably and justifiably got quite annoyed and probably would have complained. Yet, because this happened incrementally over a couple of years, it's only when I reflect back on my 'good old charging days' that I realise how inefficient my phone currently is.

---

[13] https://www.bbc.co.uk/news/science-environment-58859105

The same is happening to our natural world: We have stopped noticing the reduced number of flies on our windscreens during the summer months, or the dwindling numbers of worms in our soil, as well as the lack of butterflies fluttering around the flowers - all because it is happening so gradually.

I wanted to explore projects that not only connected us to nature, but also actively shared how to increase our awareness as well as how to best support its revival.

Fun

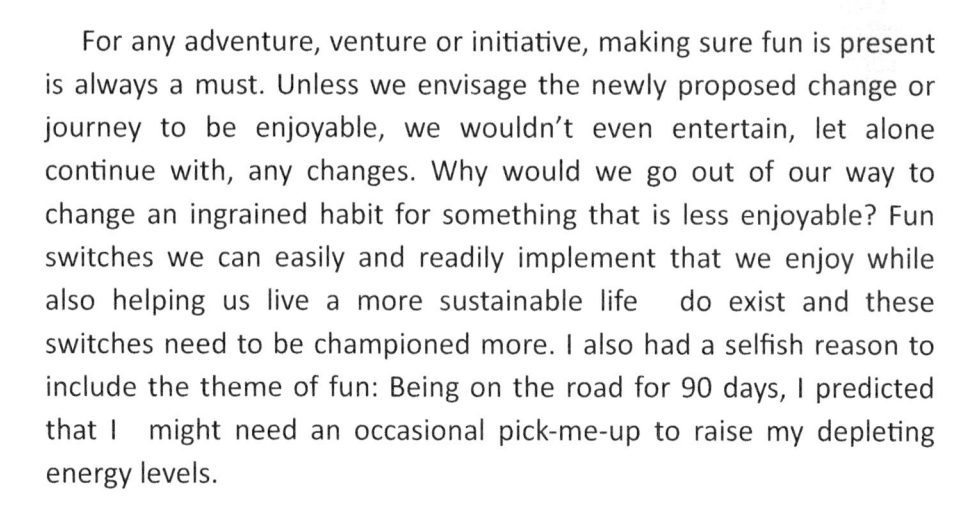

For any adventure, venture or initiative, making sure fun is present is always a must. Unless we envisage the newly proposed change or journey to be enjoyable, we wouldn't even entertain, let alone continue with, any changes. Why would we go out of our way to change an ingrained habit for something that is less enjoyable? Fun switches we can easily and readily implement that we enjoy while also helping us live a more sustainable life do exist and these switches need to be championed more. I also had a selfish reason to include the theme of fun: Being on the road for 90 days, I predicted that I might need an occasional pick-me-up to raise my depleting energy levels.

Kit

Knowing that I would be quite hypocritical of me to buy new kit for this cycle, especially when I already have drawers filled with sports clothes and equipment, I chose to wear cycling clothes I already owned and only accepted a few additional T-shirts and leggings from two clothing brands, both of whom ethically source their fabrics:

Mocean Fitness and BAM clothing. Yet, I was missing the one key item essential to complete a cycle tour: I didn't have a bike.

Having never completed a cycle tour before, with my longest cycles only being one-day events, the two bikes I own weren't fit for purpose. I have a single-speed (no gear) steel bike that I use for commuting small distances. I also had a time-trial bike from my olden days of competing in triathlon and now used for either indoor training or to loan out to cyclists curious about getting into triathlon.

Until a few years ago I did have a green road bike that was a Christmas present when I was 18 years old. Yet, alas, one Sunday, while attending church to listen to a Tibetan Buddhist speak about karma, my beautiful bike was stolen. The irony was not lost on me, but it took a few months to turn my tears of sadness into smiles of humour.

Is there a way I could use my bicycle as a practical demonstration of what is possible by putting sustainability first?

I believe that the only way to build a truly sustainable system is from the ground up. By deconstructing our current actions and critiquing every element, we are then able to discover the greenest option without impacting overall performance.

I wanted a bike that was comfortable, able to support my heavy bags carrying my kit, and also be able to survive over 3,000 miles on the road. The frame seemed the obvious choice to explore innovative materials and I found a local bike company that built frames out of bamboo.

My dream was to build and ride a frame that I made with my own hands, but after ten weeks of me cutting, sanding and glueing together bamboo pieces, I somehow failed and my frame was unrideable. Disappointed, but not deterred, I decided that this frame could be repurposed as a side-table. Fortunately, a local bike mechanic offered to build me a frame out of bamboo that was rideable.

I also stumbled upon UPSO, a bike bag manufacturer that doesn't use recycled materials, but uses something much more innovative for their fabric.

Items made from '100% recycled materials' are better than using 'recyclable' materials - at least the product isn't using 'virgin' materials. But a lot of energy is still required in converting a 'recyclable' plastic bottle into a 'recycled' T-shirt.

I personally think that repurposing materials that don't require any form of high-energy transformation is the way to go. This is what UPSO does: Using discarded truck tarp - the waterproof curtain covering the lorry's contents - they cut and sew the tarp into bike touring bags.

The material is already waterproof and, aside from a few sewing machines to stitch the material together, minimal energy input is required to make the bags: A win for me, and for the environment!

I did buy some new kit, such as a light-weight tent and sleeping bag, but I minimised the new kit as much as possible. To ensure my clothes outlived the tour, I printed a QR code that directed interested parties to a web page, instead of directly printing the details of the tour. I could always reuse my tops for future adventures and the QR code could be redirected to a different website.

The Climate Cycle wasn't about being perfect, an impossible goal that only guarantees disappointment and failure. I wanted to demonstrate ways we can all improve and also offer a layer of transparency in the solutions I had found. I also knew that I had a lot more to learn, and was looking forward to hearing from people en route, and online, how I could keep up my progress regarding the other elements of my kit and ride.

Motivation

As I spent hours planning the cycle route, organising site visits for projects and seeking accommodation options, I had to make sure that my motivation, my North Star, wasn't being squeezed out by too much planning. There needed to be space left for accidental meetings, for chance-encounters and random possibilities to happen.

For me, the Climate Cycle's North Star was *connection*.

If I planned too little, I might need to cycle further than comfortable and possibly risk injury, or find myself without food or accommodation, or possibly worse.
Yet, if I planned too much, there would be no space for exploration and those chance encounters I was curious to have.

It was a fine balance, and one I would need to constantly adjust throughout the cycle, recalibrating how much I planned against how much freedom I wanted on an almost weekly basis.

High expectations set you up for high disappointment

I know that cycling for three months wouldn't be a stroll in the park, yet I was hugely unprepared for the enormity of the reality of this tour.

On Monday 5th June 2023, World Environment Day, bleary eyed from not having enough sleep the night before, I arrived at Parliament Square in London. Leaning my bike against Winston Churchill's statue, I stamped my feet trying to stay warm in the unseasonably cool morning.

As mentioned earlier, I wanted to engage as many people in the conversation around climate change as possible and had made public all my cycle routes and publicly invited anyone to join me for the cycle, with my motto being: One hour, one day, one week, all are welcome.

Hesitantly looking around, I didn't know whether to expect one or one hundred people. My heart hoped for hundreds, but the reality of knowing people's lives were already bursting with other obligations and distractions. I would be okay with seeing just the one friend already keeping me company, Dennis, who let me stay on his sofa the night before.

'Cold isn't it?' Dennis part asked, part stated the truth.

'Mmmm' I responded, trying to ignore my concern that I was already wearing all my warm clothes and still feeling the cold wind pierce my skin.

Gradually, two more friends on bikes arrived, both conveniently called Graham.

08:05, I nodded to my small tribe of merry cyclists, pressed <start> on my Garmin that doubled up as a map as well as a tracker, and I started to slowly cycle. The Climate Cycle had officially started.

After a few hours, my band of merry kin slowly dropped off one by one, leaving me alone and with time to contemplate what was ahead of me. Almost every day for two years, I had been planning and preparing for this moment, the start of the Climate Cycle. In all honesty, it felt a little bit underwhelming because nothing much had actually changed. I was still the same 'Kate' as only days before, just without a fixed address. The world hadn't shifted, cars weren't driving slower, nor had the clouds parted to bask me in dappled sunlight to brighten my path. It was just another ordinary day.

Weather

Britain is known for its temperate climate, but even our traditionally uninspiring weather has recently been experiencing some pretty concerning peaks and troughs in our rainfall and heat. In

2022, Britain officially recorded its first ever +40°C (104°F) day, breaking the hottest day on record by a whopping 1.6°C (3°F)[14]. For 2023, the global temperature increase was confirmed at 1.18oC above average[15].

It appears that the only constant with our current weather is its unpredictability. I didn't know what to expect or what to prepare for. I was hoping for warm and dry days, avoiding any extremes, be it in temperature or precipitation.

I had hoped for mild days of dappled sunlight and light breezes (preferably tailwinds) to keep me refreshed. Yet, in 2023 - the year of my cycle - June experienced the hottest temperatures on record, and due to the shifting rainfall patterns,March, July and October were the sixth wettest months ever recorded for their respective months. In August, I also had the pleasure of cycling through two storms, Antoni and Betty.

Within a few days into my ride the cool, overcast days dissipated and I was met with two weeks of glaringly hot weather, broken only with a forceful headwind, putting more pressure on my fatiguing legs.

After three days of the sun beating down on me, apart from some extreme tan lines that were forming, I realised that my ears had blistered from the relentless sun beating down on them as I cycled. They itched and hurt when I rubbed them, and no matter how much cream I applied, they throbbed, exuding heat in the evenings. Never had I ever burned to the point of blistering, and this included the time when I competed in triathlons under the harsh Australian sun. Was this a sign of how the remaining 86 days, and future British summers, would be?

---

[14] https://www.metoffice.gov.uk/about-us/press-office/news/weather-and-climate/2022/july-heat-review
[15] https://www.climate.gov/news-features/understanding-climate/climate-change-global-temperature

If I was struggling in June with the intense sun, how were countries coping further south than us? What would happen to the tomatoes I loved eating, bought from our supermarkets, but mostly grown in Spain? And would this spark any more fires in an already damaged Greece? Would people be forced to move and find new places to call home, relocating from the threat of fires and inhospitable lands?

My blistered ears felt minimal compared to the collateral damage we collectively faced during this ever-warming summer.

The relentless sun beat down upon my back and neck as I slowly worked my way up the east coast of England towards my first day of rest: Edinburgh.

Knowing that I had two weeks of cycling without one day's rest, and coupled with the sun sucking any remaining energy from my skin and muscles, I dragged myself forward, one wheel rotation at a time.

One of the bigger concerns around the weather was less how I would be able to continue cycling through this unprecedented heat wave, especially if it got hotter and dryer, but that the weather, generally, is so unpredictable and becoming more extreme.

Britain's temperate climate of 'not too much or too little' of sunshine, rain, wind or snow ensures that our rolling countryside scenes are kept a plush green. Yet, the impact of climate change on even our predictable cluster of islands means that we can no longer depend upon any weather pattern without a growing level of uncertainty.

Climate Cycle's mission was to experience the impact of climate change within the island I call home. Climate change is happening right here and right now, with the flooding, famine, and ferocious heatwaves only set to be more consistent and more extreme.

For Climate Cycle, gratefully, the relentless sun and heat transitioned into wet relief where, on 30 June, it started to rain and it didn't stop until I reached Cornwall, nearly six weeks later.

While plodding through puddles as I navigated the damp roads, I realised that some of the initial areas I cycled through might already be flooded, and had I attempted to cycle my route just one month later, I may have been forced to stop. The majority of the Lancashire coastline is predicted to be underwater if we reach an average increase of 1.5°C (3°F) for global temperatures. This puts cities such as Hull, Skegness, Peterborough and even some boroughs of London under risk of increased sea level rises.

Recalling the hundreds of new-build houses I saw being erected along this 'danger-flood zone' in Boston, Lincolnshire brought a tear to my eye. Who was sharing the news to the future residents that these houses might not be covered by flood insurance in as little as 5 years' time?

The rain blended with my tears as I was forced to cycle through the bitter cold and wet that offered me no respite from my dark and gloomy thoughts.

The first week of wet July was one of my loneliest weeks I have ever experienced. Having just left a beautiful bunkhouse being lovingly renovated using discarded building material by a small tribe of dedicated vegans, I had felt welcomed and accepted. They had little to offer in the space of luxury and material possessions, but they had opened up their home generously and had fed and housed me for two nights.

Stretching out in front of me for the next five days was a windy, undulating road that connected the popular Fort William with the city of Glasgow. Dozens of caravaners, eager to arrive at their next destination, as well as motorcyclists taking advantage of the open and twisting roads, mingled with cars and lorries, all competing with me - the only cyclist I saw over the five days - for space on the road.

For this week, I needed to cycle 55 miles every day to make a deadline for an upcoming project visit. Typically, this would have taken me close to six hours due to my heavily laden bags, yet I was forced to stop every few hundred metres, letting the backlog of traffic pass. I spent upwards of eight hours each day standing, sitting or cycling along the road in the relentless rain. Within minutes of cycling, my clothes were saturated with water, with little streams running down my legs, slowly filling up my shoes.

I forgot to pack gloves for my cycle, naively believing that the weather would be kinder, and at the end of most days, unable to feel my fingers, before changing gears, I was forced to heat up my fingertips in my mouth.

For five whole days, I was rained upon, and with every hill that took hours to painfully crawl up, the downhill was far too quickly replaced with yet another hill. Apart from the rare view of a distant and dramatic loch, when the rain clouds parted, I had no other distractions. My earbuds wouldn't work in the rain, so instead of having music or an audiobook as company, I was left with my inner thoughts chattering away over and over and over again.

Stats that I had researched prior to my cycle about the increasingly critical predicament we, as individuals and as a nation face, engulfed me.

Human-induced activity has already contributed to warming the planet by 1.1°C (2°F), which has caused unprecedented shifts in our weather and habitat loss. With the trajectory of us predictably reaching an increase of 1.5°C (3°F)[16] over 950 million people currently live on land that will be under water stress, heat stress, and

---

[16] https://science.nasa.gov/climate-change/effects/

desertification, while in other areas flooding exposure is also predicted to impact 24% of the global population.

Not only did 2023 bring over 38 days of the highest recorded temperatures, but also sea surface temperatures reached record highs for four months, contributing to the drastic shrinkage of Antarctic sea ice, which sits around a million square kilometres smaller than the previous record[17].

And climate change isn't just a weather and species extinction concern. Escalating human crises, such as armed conflicts and economic downturns, are also predicted to accelerate, with the number of people already in humanitarian need surging to over 339 million, up from 81 million in 2014. The impacts of climate change, such as prolonged rains leading to catastrophic food insecurity in Somalia and Ethiopia, underscore the urgent need for climate change prevention and mitigation[18].

Change isn't coming, it's already here. The impact on Britain might be lagging behind other countries, such as Somalia, but it's already knocking at our door and is set to break it down soon.

While cycling, I didn't know how to stop these stats from swirling around me, so I just let go. I surrendered to the misery and sadness I was feeling. For anyone passing me, they might have thought me wild and insane: One minute I would be sobbing for the loss of our beautiful butterflies, realising that many species won't be able to recover from their dramatic declining numbers, and within a few seconds, I'd be manically laughing after a brief, but fun downhill, feeling the cold rain hit my exposed face.

My emotions were as undulating as the road I cycled upon.

---

[17] https://www.wri.org/insights/2023-ipcc-ar6-synthesis-report-climate-change-findings
[18] https://www.nhm.ac.uk/discover/news/2023/october/climate-change-reaching-unprecedented-levels-records-tumble.html

Glasgow arrived not a minute too soon, and I limped towards the home of a Doctor I had never met in person, but knew through Plant-Based Health Professionals, an organisation offering education and support for medical professionals - and patients - wishing to complement their healthcare with lifestyle changes.

Sustenance

Being plant-based is a lot easier now than when I first transitioned to this lifestyle 10 years' ago, but it still proves tricky, especially while travelling. Being on the road and not having my own cooking utensils, I didn't have the luxury of being able to prepare my own meals and I had to rely on whatever was on offer at local convenience stores.

I felt that the more remote the region, the more expensive the natural and wholefoods foods were in comparison to the processed foods. One afternoon, stopping at a small independent shop in the north east of England, I craved the crunch and sweet taste of an apple. Scouring the aisles, not one apple was to be found, yet at the end of the fridge, I could see a crisp red pepper glinting in the shop's stark lighting.

'Yum' I thought as I tottered my way towards the red goodness and, as I picked it up, mouth already salivating from imagining the first bite of this vegetable, I saw the price. Confused, I looked nearby to find the other red peppers, not believing that one single pepper would cost £2.50, yet this was the truth.

Behind me, a 500g packet of crisps was £1.50 and a packet of ginger biscuits was £1.75. Being mindful of budget, as I wasn't earning an income during my ride, and even though I had some financial sponsors, their generous support didn't cover the total cost of the ride. I feared that these daily 'snack stops' were getting expensive.

Reluctantly putting down the red pepper, I picked up the biscuits, knowing that even though they were the unhealthy option, they would fill me up for longer.

I craved home-cooked plant-based food and Dr Hayley Tait's stay in Glasgow didn't disappoint. Waiting for me in her family home was some delicious vegetable stir fry that I sat down and enjoyed with her family., The nourishing food calmed my nerves and with each mouthful, I felt more at ease. With Hayley, her husband and two young children, we shared   stories of our experiences with climate change and health concerns that led each of us to turn to food as part of our medicine, and a solution to reducing our personal impact on the world. 'Please, start from the beginning,' I mumbled between mouthfuls, inviting Hayley to keep talking as I went back for a third helping of her delicious food.

Throughout my three months on the road, I noticed a shift in my body composition. During the entire 90 days, I lost about 5kg (11 pounds) of weight and I also toned up significantly, especially around my waist and arms. The residual layer of 'lockdown fat', I was still carrying after taking up cold water swimming and needing more insulation to warm me, had been burned off in the many miles and, even though muscles weren't showing, I had more contours and shape in these areas.

What surprised me was how my palette changed over the three months. For me, I was eating an excessive amount of heavily processed food, where most days I would eat a dozen biscuits and at least one packet of crisps. Upon the completion of the cycle, without exception, I had to add more salt to every dish before tasting the flavours. I also felt the addictive and compulsive urge to eat crisps and other high-fat foods, missing the feel and flavour. It took a few months to deliberately remove biscuits from my reach, and gradually wean myself off the crisps too.

Be in the question

The focus of the Climate Cycle was to highlight the communities and projects I was visiting during the cycle.

The topic of climate and sustainability can be overwhelming and encompasses every single element of life. From the moment we wake up, every action we take and item we touch has an environmental impact. From our energy provider, supplying us the electricity we use to power our alarm clock, to the bulb that is in our bedside table, it is impossible to hide from the footprint our decisions leave behind.

In order for there to be a semblance of sanity and cohesion within the projects I visited, I decided to focus on what I personally feel are the areas we individually have the most control over. There is little use in visiting manufacturers of car batteries, or meeting with members of parliament who write policies, because most of us don't have a sway or the means to influence these activities. But we can choose what we eat, what we buy, the way we travel, and how we interact with our natural environment.

I focused on actions we could implement simply and easily with little disruption to our daily lives because, in honesty, aren't we all a bit too busy to be adding yet another thing to think about into our already full days?

One lasting passion I discovered during my five years of studying engineering is my love of spreadsheets. Opening up a blank screen, filled with little boxes, waiting to be populated with numbers, words and formulas is guaranteed to put a smile on my face. The concept that a wild and disorganised idea can somehow be tamed and put into order excites me. Climate Cycle needed a master sheet that encompassed multiple projects over a variety of themes, as well as every project being located in a different location and time-sensitive. I was ready to take on this complex challenge, and enjoyed researching different charities and companies throughout Britain.

One project I was particularly looking forward to was to visit a seagrass field in North Wales managed by the charity Project Seagrass. From first glance, this project clearly sat in the theme of 'nature-based solutions'. Seagrass is a carbon-absorber, holding up to four times more carbon than trees. It also acts as a natural storm barrier, preventing sand being washed downstream and reducing coastal erosion in high and stormy tides. Seagrass is also a nursery for a plethora of marine wildlife.It is common to see fish to sharks as well as seals using the seagrass fields as a place to lay eggs and raise their young.

Yet, it didn't take much reading for me to realise that increasing the amount of seagrass fields along the British shore wouldn't just benefit the marine ecology and protect the beaches from storm damage, it also helps increase fish population, it offers a fun activity for children to play in the seagrass, and as a fun holiday activity, we're able to volunteer in collecting and replanting the seagrass seeds! In short, the simple topic of seagrass covered four of my five themes.

And again, this is a good reminder that life isn't about living under a certain title or 'identity' - just like each of us plays many roles in our lives, so too do these projects. I am a daughter, mentor, friend, athlete, author, lover, business consultant, geek, and many more, so why limit seagrass to just one description?

The only way to work towards mitigating the climate crisis is to work together and allow the solution to emerge. There isn't one 'answer', because - just like these projects - it's complicated with many overlaps.

I knew I had to let go of my desire to know everything and surrender to the journey, trusting that the best way to tackle climate change would be revealed through my willingness to stay 'in the question', rather than force an outcome.

The thread connecting the projects

My greatest desire was to meet with people from as diverse walks of life as possible. My dream was that the day my cycle was announced, people would organically come and join me, culminating in numbers until, on the last day, hundreds of people would cycle into London, finishing at Parliament Square to an announcement that the government had listened to us and was addressing some of our climate concerns.

Being on the road for 90 days and nights, even though I was carrying a tent, I also wanted - and needed - to rely on the hospitality of strangers, giving me access to a shower and possibly a place to occasionally wash my clothes. I'm not averse to infrequent washing, or wearing the same top for a few days, but I was mindful of the people I would be visiting, especially the schools. Children would have no barrier in telling me if I turned up smelly!

My original plan for the Climate Cycle was to wild camp at every occasion. My conviction for this plan was so strong that I carried the additional weight of a tent and sleeping bag to make sure that I could sleep under the stars as much as possible. Yet, this was not meant to be. I only camped for 14 nights, with close to two thirds of my nights leaning on the generosity of strangers. I camped much less than I had hoped due to three core factors:

Worry: At the time of me cycling, the last remaining legal location to wild camp in England and Wales had been lost. This meant that any camping outside of an official campsite and without the explicit permission of the landowner was deemed illegal. I could be in a remote location of the Dorset moors, at a secluded beach in Cornwall, or next to a country road behind a hedge and I could be fined and run the risk of being moved on.

It didn't matter if I left no trace of me camping and took all my litter with me, it was still seen as me breaking the law.

Scotland has a very different view on our access to nature, and allows individuals to wild camp anywhere they desire.

One charity organisation, Right To Roam, feels that the 'no wild camping' rule in England and Wales creates a barrier from us exploring natural areas. We rarely protect what we don't like, and we don't like what we don't know. Maybe if more people camped next to a forest, river, or meadow, we would have more people caring when these areas are lost or polluted?

Yet even with my desire to camp and connect with these natural areas, I am still a stickler for rules, and carried a fear that if I did pitch my tent in a discrete area behind a hedgerow, someone may see me and force me to move on, or worse, call the police and have me arrested.

This worry would have affected the quality of my sleep, always playing on my mind as I tried to drift off, that I might have a jolt in waking up and need to pack up and cycle in the middle of the night.

Weariness: The second reason why camping became a larger challenge for me was my physical exhaustion. I hadn't factored that I would be so tired from cycling for most of the day. The thought of spending the better part of one hour to stop, unpack and pitch my tent, and secure my bike and belongings every evening, as well as another hour required to pack up my tent and get ready to cycle, filled my heart with dread. Those two hours each day could be spent sleeping, resting, preparing my maps, or confirming my upcoming project visits.

I was too tired to spend time organising my sleeping situation and desired a simpler, more efficient, means of resting.

Weather: The one constant these past few years have shown is that the weather is inconsistent. I didn't know what I would be cycling into, and I had a shock with July being one of the wettest Julys Britain had ever experienced.

Waking up to the sound of raindrops hitting the outside of my tent, putting on damp clothes that didn't dry in the cold conditions, as well as packing an already drenched tent into a damp bag, was miserable. After two days of wringing my socks out from the excess water before forcing my toes back into the cold and clingy cloth, I gave up changing my clothes, rationalising that I was going to get wet within a few short minutes, so why bother changing at all.

I had no means of warming myself up, washing or drying my clothes, nor a place to allow my tent to recover from the previous night's downpour, Mentally, I was struggling to enjoy the cycle, knowing that in the evening I would be cramped into a tent too small to sit up in, surrounded by my possessions getting more and more waterlogged.

I gave up on my idealistic idea of camping and surrendered to my situation. It was more important to stay mentally positive, free from illness due to being so cold and wet over many days of rain, and to find other - warmer and dryer - places to sleep.

Warm Showers is a gorgeous community of individuals wanting to help people just like me enjoy their adventures a little more.

During my cycle, I stayed in over 40 different homes. One couple in Inverness wanted to practise their hospitality skills, and patience, with travellers before embarking on opening a Bed and breakfast. Another retired couple were avid cyclists and had recently returned from a tandem tour of Route 66 in the States, where they had benefited from the hospitality of strangers and were now giving back to the travelling community.

After a particularly hard few weeks on the road, I asked a couple in Dorset if I could extend my stay and enjoy a rest day at their home, to which they readily agreed and offered to wash my clothes.

My heart warmed to the generosity of these strangers; people who offered me so much even when some may not have had much themselves. One lady, who lived in a caravan, shared her evening dinner and let me stay on her lounge floor, so I didn't have to camp in the rain for another night.

Apart from the obvious benefits of a warm place to sleep, the possibility of a shower, and, on nearly every occasion, a meal to enjoy, there was also an accidental benefit of staying with 'strangers'; I could open up the conversation of climate change and hear their views and thoughts on this topic.

How important is climate change to them? What actions, if anything, did they engage with? Whose responsibility was it to take action over mitigating the crisis? What are their views on climate activists and organisations such as Extinction Rebellion (XR) and Just Stop Oil? And, was my cycle making any impact at all in the climate conversation?

My narrow perception on climate change started broadening to include differing solutions, viewpoints and methods tackling this sometimes seemingly overwhelming topic.

Even though I secretly wished that everyone I met, be it a cyclist or host, would share similar views around the urgency of action to mitigate climate change, this was not always the case.

One such case was when my cycle companion for one day in the North East of England took it upon himself to point out every closed mine we passed, lamenting the loss of such an important part of the community's past.

'And look,' he proudly stated, pointing at a monstrous building that sat on the side of a river. 'They've just opened a new concrete factory, putting our area back on the map.' Two large chimneys emitted relentless clouds of white smoke and I paused in silence, realising that he was honestly happy to have this heavy polluting factory as a part of his town.

My heart sank a little, because I could see the reason why he was so happy; jobs had been created and a 'better' future successfully sold to the community.

Yet, at what cost?

A town that had welcomed a steel factory into its sleepy South Welsh community, Port Talbot, initially welcomed the influx of well paid jobs, improved roads and the possibility of dreaming bigger than an agricultural profession. But it became quickly apparent that all was not 'rainbows and butterflies'. With this area having a life expectancy up to 3.5 years less than most other Welsh regions, was this linked with the pollution being generated from the steel factory?[19]

There seems to be a missing piece to the story about why the media and governments tend to focus on the profitability aspect of 'sustainability' and either downplay or ignore the impact of the environment and longer-term consequences for future generations in these areas. Do governments value more economic sustainability and growth over personal health and stability? And why is our natural world, the silent lungs and creators of our life, the least of all considered?

I wasn't angered or frustrated by this man's comments concerning the cement factory, only a little saddened because he was looking at the factory from one very narrow angle. Yes, jobs and a means to earn a living is critical for us, yet not at the cost of our health and future wellbeing.

Was there a possibility that, on the same site, a factory could have generated a similar number of jobs through the manufacture of eco bricks repurposing single-use plastic destined for landfill?

Not only would the traditional engineering jobs be protected, but this could also offer the opportunity to create a completely new and much more eco-friendly way of manufacturing raw materials for the building industry?

But, this was never on offer, so the way we've always done it won yet again.

---

[19] https://statswales.gov.wales/Catalogue/Health-and-Social-Care/Life-Expectancy/LifeExpectancy-by-LocalAuthority-Gender

The air we breathe

I may have been less sympathetic to the economic impact on this region by the mine closures because of a chance meeting with an air quality expert a few days before my departure.

I had visited The Global Centre for Clean Air Research, GCARE, at the University of Surrey. Expecting a quick tour of their facilities and a few photos before cycling back home, I was pleasantly surprised to be greeted by the entire team, comprising PhD students and staff. At some point during the three and a half hours of deep discussion, which ranged from how air quality, both indoors and outside, can impact more than our health, to methods to absorb and reduce the pollution through strategic planting of different fauna, I impulsively said 'wouldn't it be great if I could track my air as I cycled?', not expecting them to respond positively.

'What a great idea, Kate!' Professor Prashant chimed, with Ana, a PhD graduate quickly agreeing.

'You can carry a small device on your bike and each evening send us the data to analyse,' they confirmed.

With just a few days before my departure, I received a small black rectangular cube-shaped device that could be strapped on the outside of my pannier bags. This would be tracking various air quality parameters as I cycled around Britain.

Now that I had an air tracking device with me, I became acutely aware of the cars, buses and lorries that drove alongside me, and the fumes that I could see being chuffed out of their exhausts and straight into my lungs - and the air tracking device. I'm sure that I couldn't see the exhaust fumes, and it was just my imagination creating the disturbing images of small black particles slowly descending around me, being breathed in and slowly covering the inside of my lungs, restricting my oxygen intake and, with every single breath, slowly reducing my health and shortening my lifespan.

Unconsciously, at traffic lights, I'd cover my mouth or, at the least, turn my head away from the neighbouring vehicles.

Girls (even climate-aware ones) just want to have fun

The projects along the cycle tour, which aimed to reduce our contribution to the acceleration of climate change and mitigate its impact on our lives and the natural environment, were meant to dominate my cycle tour - not the weather.

I wanted to explore these projects and discover first-hand how they were engaging with their communities and neighbours. Were people unaware of the project's existence, or did they choose to conveniently ignore the 'wild and crazy greenie projects' on the peripheries of their village or town?

An enthusiast of behavioural change, I adore exploring the inertia of people who say that they care about a cause, and yet still don't change behaviour. One such example is organ donation. In England, prior to 2020, it was an optional opt-in for adults to donate their organs after their passing, and around 80% of people said that they supported organ donation in principle. Yet - and this is the figure that interests me - only 38% actually made the effort and officially recorded their decision to donate[20].

80% of the English population cared about, and agreed with, organ donation, yet less than half of those cared enough to pick up a form from the local pharmacy and commit to what they cared about.

Pick any subject in the world and there will typically be the resistors (20% in the case of organ donation[21]), and there will also be the implementers (approximately 30% of the population). The group that I lovingly refer to as the 'inert masses' accounts for the majority of society. What needs to be present for these people to form an opinion regarding this topic? Do these people not care, not care enough, are unaware, or are not motivated enough to change from the default position of inertia?

Action around climate change is more subtle. There aren't simple metrics to verify whether people have 'opted in' to not cutting their lawn until May to allow pollinators more time to feed, as one example. For simplicity, I'm going to apply my crude assumptions and percentages from organ donation opt in/out data to climate change, assuming the similar bell-shaped curve of resistors, inert masses and activators.

Is there anything that could help nudge people from inertia into caring for and engaging with climate-benefiting activities? Could some of the lesser known projects awaken these 'inert masses' - the majority of our population - and encourage them to switch from single-use coffee cups to washable and reusable mugs, and beyond?

---

[20] https://www.nhsbt.nhs.uk/news/family-urges-people-to-confirm-their-organ-donation-decision-two-years-on-from-law-change/
#:~:text=Their%20decision%20gave%20five%20patients,recorded%20their%20decision%20to%20donate

[21] For those wishing to check my maths, 38% of 80% is 30%.

Personally, I believe that there will always be 'extreme' individuals, such as myself, that are prepared to tolerate personal discomfort for the 'greater good' and for causes dear to our hearts. But the majority of people look at individuals like myself with justified wary curiosity. We aren't typical and it requires a lot of energy to wake up every day and set aside our personal comfort, such as renting a home or earning consistent income from a regular job. People like me are exceptional and extreme and should not be seen as good role models - my life is precarious, tough, and ironically unsustainable for the long-term.

When not forced upon them, such as through redundancy or divorce, most people make changes because they see a personal benefit in doing so. There are products, services, and solutions that enable us to be sustainable and climate-conscious while also being enjoyable. The fact that they don't release toxins into our waterways or fund sweatshops might be a subtle secondary benefit. Could Climate Cycle highlight the hedonistic and personally benefiting reasons for being sustainable, and focus less on the altruistic and less tangible benefits?

We're surrounded by adverts promoting the allure of a remote Caribbean beach destination, the excitement of climbing an Andean mountaintop, or enjoying the succulent tastes of a weekend getaway to a European city, forgetting that places much closer to home carry similar allure and wonder.

Britain is a playground for us to enjoy and explore, boasting long stretches of beaches, ragged rocky mountain peaks to summit as well as hamlets and cities to discover. A few years before embarking on this cycle, I visited Oxford for the first time and was in awe when I realised I was standing under the lamppost that inspired 'The Chronicles of Narnia.' Ås I walked towards the river, I discovered this meandering waterway was home to Toad of 'Toad Hall' as well as 'Alice in Wonderland'! Within 30 minutes of arriving in this city, my thoughts were flooded with cherished childhood memories of the books and stories that had played such a pivotal role in nurturing my imagination and creativity.

This one day trip opened my eyes to yet more wonder and possibility, and I had only travelled a few hours' by train from my home. What else could I be missing out from always assuming that the grass was greener abroad?

Along the cycle, in York, one couple, inspired by their long dog walks through the lavender fields, launched a clothing brand that mirrored nature's colour palette and only used fabric suppliers from Europe and 99% recycled material, limiting the carbon miles to transport the fabric, as well as ensuring a living wage and fair working conditions for their supply chain employees.

Mocean Fitness clothing not only looks and feels good, guaranteeing cute gym selfies, but also serves a practical purpose, and if consumers buy for these reasons alone, it's enough. Yet behind the scenes, the company ensures that we are doing good with every purchase regardless if that is of interest or motivation to us.

Another project that stood out to me is tackling the thousands of plastic bodyboards discarded each summer on our British beaches. Bodyboards are made of polystyrene, something very toxic and energy-demanding to produce and almost impossible to recycle.

These floating pollutants are cheap to buy and the price probably highlights the poor working conditions for those manufacturing the boards.

Side note: As a general rule of thumb, there is always a cost, and if what we're buying is cheap, then the cost is passed on somewhere else - typically either modern-slave labour, unhealthy working conditions, or environmental pollution.

I found a Cornish company making a dent on the plastic bodyboard problem by selling wooden bodyboards made from locally sourced and ethically harvested wood. During my tour of the Dick Pearce shop, which also doubles up as their manufacturing unit, I loved touching the stencils used to etch personalised messages on each board. Taking a deep breath in, the soft smell of wood calmed me and the bright colours of the boards leaning along the walls brought a smile to my face. I felt at home in this eclectic space. It didn't matter that I was wearing the same t-shirt as the previous two days, nor that I was carrying a bike bag instead of a handbag, the space welcomed you up however you turned up.

'Would you like to try a board?' Nashi, the quiet but fast-moving employee offered. 'Of course!' I replied, quickly choosing a beautifully decorated board that looked more like something I'd hang on a wall than throw into the ocean and attempt to ride a wave.

From my first independent trip while still in school, I prefer to travel alone. I was desperate to break free from the safe confines of my family home in Wales. Since I was seven years' old, I had a secret overnight bag packed with what I thought were essentials for running away. Inside the bag were my favourite T-shirt, a fresh pair of pants and socks, pen and paper to take notes on what I saw, as well as some money for bus trips. The final item was a banana used to lure my younger brother to join me. It was typically this final item that led to the discovery of my secret 'runaway' bag. After many weeks of plotting my escape, my mother would always find my sickly sweet-smelling bag of rotting bananas, and my plans would be thwarted. My brother was also very hesitant to go travelling, and no amount of bananas offered would sway his decision.

Finally, at the age of seventeen, when my parents reluctantly gave me permission to travel without their protective eye and steering hand, I planned an epic summer of adventure and cultural immersion.

A train trip across Europe called me, and even though my two best friends were planning an almost identical train trip, it never crossed my mind to travel with them.

I have enjoyed many solo trips since then, as well as trips with others, and both types of travel offer different experiences. Being alone, I am forced to - and enjoy - speaking with more people, and typically make more friends than when I'm travelling with someone else.

Yet when wanting to go bodyboarding on a wooden board, travelling with someone else is definitely a bonus. Where could I safely store my bag containing my mobile phone and clothes when I went splashing in the waves?

Cornwall in summer is a magnet for beach-loving Brits. The long, sandy beaches and promise of warm weather draws huge crowds that clog up the meandering country roads and overflow onto beaches. On the beach, families desperately try to stake a claim to a slice of tranquillity amid the chaos of other families. They scream at their partner to pitch a tent facing 'a bit more to the left, erect fabric walls, and build mini castles around what they deem their temporary land.

It isn't just families that are drawn to the sandy shores of Newquay, as groups of stags, hens, and teenagers fluctuate between dancing to very loud pop music and unsuccessfully trying to reduce the burnt red tan lines emerging from alcohol-induced siestas.

Looking around, I was nervous to leave my small but precious bag of possessions alone, partly because I might lose its location in the sea of seemingly identical groups, and partly because someone might think my possessions were valuable and take them.

The noise and apparent manic disorder swirled in my head and I could feel the knot in my stomach grow. My walk started to curve around, and I prepared to return to the shop, never having touched the water. But as I was turning around, my eyes glanced above the scattered bodies and tops of tents, and I caught sight of the watery horizon. The water stretched far beyond what I could see and looking at the rippling blue-grey ocean seemed to quieten the noise around me and slowly release the knot from my stomach.

I craved to touch the salty water, and feel its sting as well as cool freshness splash against my body and face. I had been cycling for almost two months and my body yearned for the intimate embrace of mother nature and the great blue healer.

At this point, I noticed a woman sitting under an awning while she intently watched two children play in front of her. She seemed trustworthy and I decided to slowly walk past her and assess if she'd be appropriate to watch over my possessions.

My instinct proved right and, just as I walked past, she glanced up and smiled at me.

It's in these moments of human interaction that my love for people and hope for the future is reignited. A stranger's smile, a passerby opening the door, or a fellow underground traveller offering their seat. These small acts of kindness are mini ripples of change that remind me that, on some level, the vast majority of people care, are compassionate and seek a heart-felt connection within communities and their lives. The woman's smile was a beacon of support in a sea of strangers, and gave me the opportunity to leave my bag with her as I dove into the water, washing away not just months of grime from cycling, but also my fatigue, my disenchantment. The salty water rekindled my desire to continue cycling and hopefully help highlight more causes and projects contributing towards a brighter place for us all.

Another project of 'fun' was on the opposite coast of England nestled between some low lying fields and a housing estate.

During my planning and researching phase of the Climate Cycle, I stumbled across another adventurer, Dave Cornthwaite, who quit his regular job and embarked on a life where he felt alive every day, rather than desperately wishing away his week for the glimmer of a joyous weekend.

During one of his many adventures, Dave met Em. They got married and bought a field in Lincolnshire, got a dog, some alpacas and chickens and decided to launch a festival. They also converted a double decker bus into a self-contained, 100% off grid home for travellers to come and stay.

The festival, aptly called YEStival encourages people to say 'yes' more. Say 'yes' to adventure, to being brave, to doing something different, to writing that book, or learning a new language. The festival celebrates the optimism of what is possible when we commit - sometimes naively - to disrupting the predictable path of our future and imminent boredom.

After a particularly windy cycle where, unfortunately, the wind was blowing in my face creating a tough headwind to push against, I turned down a gravel path and could see a bright blue double-decker bus sitting in the middle of a field glistened in the setting sun.

'Would you like an upgrade from a tent for tonight?' Dave generously asked. 'Of course!' I beamed, relishing the thought of not having to spend the better part of the evening unpacking my tent before being able to sleep.

'You might be woken up early by your neighbours though,' he added, nodding towards an enclosure next to the bus. I glanced over and could see half a dozen alpacas casually looking over in our direction.

'Not a problem,' I smiled back, and suppressed a small jump for joy. The bus, powered by solar panels, had a chill zone and small kitchen downstairs. Carrying my bags to the top floor, I read inspirational quotes and motivational quotes stating 'Say YES More' along the bus walls. At the top of the stairs was an overflowing bookshelf, filled with books written by people who broke the routine and embarked on bold and exciting adventures. Some books explained the technique of dragging yourself up big mountains in cold climates, while others spoke of the tropical warmth of exploring communities in exotic rainforests. One day, would I be able to contribute to this bookshelf, I mused?

Collapsing onto a double bed at the back of the bus, I wrapped myself up in my sleeping bag and fell into a very restful sleep dreaming of alpacas and adventures.

Doing the right thing doesn't have to mean limiting ourselves or cutting out things we enjoy. We just need to get a bit creative and step away from the habitual patterns and the easiest path.

Reframing a holiday to include the travel itself, as well as time on the beach, can mean we have more time to enjoy the experience. Instead of the stress of a busy airport and rushing to fly as fast as possible, we can slow down and let the journey unfold much sooner. Let the travel become part of the vacation, rather than annoying bookends that shorten our enjoyment.

My dear friend Graham decided to change his cycling adventure from exploring Vietnam with a group of strangers, to joining me on the iconic and spectacular Scottish North Coast 500. This 500-mile circular road trip passes through historic villages and a deliciously undulating stretch of rugged coast. We also kept an eye on the North Sea, which hugged the coastline, because I had heard from Steve Truluck - a whale enthusiast - that orcas and spur whales had been spotted a few days earlier along the same coastline that we were cycling.

Similar to Dave from Lincolnshire, Steve had also quit his well paid, but unsatisfying job as a civil engineer and moved to Moray, Scotland, after a brief business trip to the area. The rugged landscape of the Scottish land, and warm hearts of the locals stayed with him long after he returned to the grind of long work hours bookended with gruelling commutes and, gradually, he started questioning whether he actually had life planned the right way round.

Why was he working at the prime of his life, desperately wishing five of his seven days away to then be too tired to take advantage of his brief weekend of freedom? Wasn't life meant for more than working, bills, and commuting?

Within a few months, he handed in his notice, listed his house for sale, and gave away most of his possessions. How many jumpers and books does one person need anyway? Packing what was left of his life into his car, he drove 'up north' to truly start living a life that excited him.

Initially, he rented a caravan for a short-term solution while looking for more 'typical' accommodation to rent. During this time, he realised that he didn't need much more space than his two-wheeled home. Not having a large rent to pay meant he could commit less time to earning money and more time to the love of his life: watching whales.

On paper, Steve shouldn't have gone much further than staying a spectator to the whales' activities. Every single day, Steve wakes up feeling excited about what he might see playing on the ocean, visible from his caravan window. Due to his passion for these mammals, he has learnt their routines and rhythms, almost pre-empting where they would feed, mate, and play. His dedication has earned him respect and recognition as a self-taught whale expert. He has been featured in a documentary, and is now paid to host excursions for other whale enthusiasts. Additionally, he is regularly invited to share his knowledge, not only about whale habits, but also about ways to protect these whales from man-made risks.

I met him accidentally after watching his documentary and self-inviting myself to visit while I cycled past. His childlike wonder for the ocean is infectious and I joined him as he part ran, part fell down a sandy slope onto a beach, getting a better view of a possible whale sighting after our dinner together.

Steve reminded me that caring for something doesn't mean carrying the cause as a heavy burden, like I sometimes do. Knowing about the diminishing number of our whales and shoals of fish sits like a heavy chain around my neck, pulling me down. The guilt of not doing enough, or not speaking out at every occasion, prevents me from enjoying the small moments of joy, such as witnessing the distant spray of a whale as she surfaces for air.

It's important to keep pushing for what we care about, but it's unsustainable without allowing there to be moments to let our hair down and enjoy what we currently have too.

Keep the goal in stone and the journey in sand

We don't know what we don't know. This statement was especially true for my preparation and training leading up to the Climate Cycle. Having only cycled for 24 hours in one sitting on a stationary bike and camped - with my bike - for just one night away, I had no idea what to expect or what I needed to have in place - mentally, physically, or emotionally - to support me for 90 days on the road.

I thought that, over my three years of planning, I had considered every eventuality and sought counsel from a vast array of individuals. Their words of advice, based on their lived experiences, set me up to be as prepared as possible.

There's a fine line between over-planning to the point of sucking the joy out of a project - turning an initial spark of excitement into a burden of concern and fear of possible eventualities - and also being borderline ignorant, loosely disguised as naive or innocent.

After my first failed attempt at the static cycling 24-hour world record in 2017, I sometimes still felt the shadow of embarrassment and slight guilt that I hadn't trained effectively enough and didn't deliver on my commitment to my volunteers. They had committed a sleepless night to support me, and I felt I had let them down due to my lack of preparation and training. This judgement never came from others, I am my biggest critic.

I didn't want the Climate Cycle to be another list of my 'naive mistakes', yet also knew that it was almost impossible to train for such an extreme distance.

The original plan was to cycle 3,000 miles around the coastline of England, Scotland, and Wales, through counties and regions known for their hills. Whenever I shared my route, the response I received, without exception, was always 'it's hilly in […],' with the hilliest location changing with every answer. I had the Scottish highlands to navigate, the majestic Lake District to flow through, as well as the undulating Welsh coastline and Cornish hills to look forward to.

And the counties and regions between these well-known hilly areas offered their own challenges, with extreme weather conditions, busy roads, and barely a flat road in sight!

My physical training consisted of long, slow rides four to five times a week, with at least one ride reaching double-digits in hours. This allowed for my body - especially my bottom - to become used to sitting on the saddle for extended periods of time. It didn't matter how far I cycled because I knew that my body could push onwards, on the proviso that I wasn't struggling with injury or chafing.

Being hyper flexible, my default position is to lock my joints in place, rather than rely on the strength of my muscles. By locking my elbows and lower back it creates a tension and ricochet effect, where the jarring from cycling jolts upwards and into larger joints, typically manifesting in intense pain.

And my crotch (I have never spoken so much nor so publicly about my crotch since I took up endurance cycling!) is a very sensitive spot that carries my entire weight while cycling. Every single rotation of my legs, where I average 82 rotations per minute, creates heat and also the potential to rub some very delicate skin.

I not only carried the emotional scars of my failed world record attempt, but I also had more recent physical wounds from the successful attempt a few years' ago. After many hours of spinning, I chafed so badly that I was cycling on open wounds, with my skin ripped apart. My poor physio had the unenviable task of briefly laying me down to apply glue and stick my broken skin together, enabling me to keep on cycling until the end of the 24 hours.

For the Climate Cycle, a big part of my focus was on chafe elimination and back/elbow strengthening. Hiring a personal trainer, Tao, we devised a training plan to strengthen my core, biceps, and triceps to override my natural desire to lock my joints, and to activate my muscle groups instead. These three months of weekly sessions proved invaluable, and my back and arms were two of the only places that didn't hurt by the end of the cycle!

Yet, even working with a trainer, I hadn't even considered that any other body part might fail, or the immense toll cycling for so long would have on my fatigue, energy and emotional levels.

Rationalising that I wanted to cover more distance in the first month, I set the target of completing half the total distance within four weeks. The mental relief of knowing that I would be over halfway would prove a significant morale boost to my motivation. Additionally, as my fatigue increased, I could reduce the number of miles and hours spent cycling. On paper, the theory makes sense, and based on this I planned for my first rest day to be in Edinburgh, twelve days of cycling and 690 miles (1,787 km) away from London.

Within three days of my cycle, a small knot of dread in the pit of my stomach increasingly grew as the realisation that I had maybe set too ambitious a target, and my carefully thought-out plan might backfire.

On paper, it made sense to delay my first day of rest until I had made an impressive dent in the route. Yet, I hadn't factored in the additional burden on my body carrying the 30 kg of kit. With every push uphill, my knees started to creak and groan a little bit more.

In addition to the physical discomfort of my knees feeling like they had grains of sharp shards of glass in them, the many hours of cycling alone while tired, as well as knowing that I had more than two thousand miles yet to cover, slowly added a residual layer of foreboding. Even on the sunny days, a grey filter of concern reduced the immediate gratification of reaching a viewpoint or top of a hill. 'Don't get too excited,' my inner critic would warn. 'This is only the tip of the iceberg of pain waiting for you' this annoying voice chimed.

The only guarantee to silence my inner critic was when I had company join me on the ride. Even with my most valiant attempts at inviting people to join me, I had been cycling alone since leaving Norfolk, day three of my tour. I created a dedicated web page listing my entire route, which had been hand-designed with the help of Graham. The tour had also been announced to members of British Cycling and Cycling UK. Yet, despite these efforts, I found myself mostly alone for the majority of my ride.

At the beginning, this solitude was the hardest to process, partly because my expectations were high. I had dreamt that I would be akin to the Forest Gump of cycling and amass dozens, if not hundreds, of like minded cyclists wishing to use their bike as a vehicle (excuse the pun) for change regarding the climate crisis.

Waking up each morning, I would open the private WhatsApp group and check for confirmations of people joining me. Within the group, I typically read many words of encouragement, yet for over two-thirds of the days, I cycled alone, with no company to speak with or join me.

Leaving England into Scotland, the weather was particularly intense with sharp and uncharacteristically hot weather beating down on my back. With every hour under the relentless glare of the sunlight, not only was the skin on my ears and forearms slowly drying, burning, and peeling away, but so too was my desire to continue. Within 25 miles of arriving in Edinburgh, and my first rest day off the bike, my mind had already given up, craving a soft mattress, dark curtains, and no alarm clock to wake me in the morning. It felt as if time was standing still and no matter how often I glanced at my computer, the distance barely seemed to change between checks. The more tired I became, the slower I cycled, and the more I found myself looking down at my computer, wishing that the screen would miraculously show that I had cycled the full distance to get to my much-craved rest.

As the road widened, replacing trees with signs of suburbia, I heard the unmistakable sound of a cyclist freewheeling behind me. The tick-tick-tick of their wheel cut through the windless day and from the corner of my eye, I could see two middle aged men dressed in lycra (lovingly referred to as MAMLs in cycle terminology) gently catching me up.

From my slumped shoulders, they probably guessed that I was struggling, and without uttering a word, they slowed their pace to cycle alongside me.

Grateful that neither asked me where I cycled from, nor what was my destination, I didn't need to relive the hundreds of tiresome miles that I had dragged myself through to get to this moment.

'Did you know that this village was the first to...' The older of the two guys stated as we reached a hamlet. I don't recall where we were, nor what the fact was, but it was a welcome distraction. He continued talking and pointing at road signs and distant church spires. I knew what he was doing, he was distracting me from what was evident to all - I was almost bonking, or 'hitting the wall' as it's also known, and I needed to focus on something other than my imminent demise.

I've only ever bonked once before, and it's not pleasant. The first time I ever experienced it was when I had just arrived at a training camp on the volcanic island of Lanzarote. Eager to experience all that this island had to offer, within three minutes of arriving I unpacked my bike, threw on my lycra and helmet and went out for a quick 'spin around the block.' I didn't take any water or food with me because I only imagined that I'd be, at the most, half an hour on the road.

Even though it was early spring, the sun was fierce, and within 10 minutes I realised that not only was the temperature significantly warmer than any summer ride I had attempted back in the UK, but by my parched mouth, I sensed that the climate was also a lot dryer.

In my haste, I had forgotten to memorise neither the address of my hotel, nor the twists and turns I initially took to reach the coastal road.

For over three hours, I cycled in ever-decreasing circles, desperation growing as I searched for my hotel and solace from the relentless sun. My legs felt as though they were turning to lead, and even blinking was becoming too much to manage. Fortunately, before anything serious happened, I recognised a side-street that quickly led to my hotel. Exhausted and barely able to stand, I collapsed into my hotel room, half-falling, half-crawling towards the bathroom. There, I filled the sink with cold water and splashed it against my burning skin while immersing my head into the crisp water, taking gulps of this precious elixir.

Just outside Edinburgh, the second cyclist discreetly passed me his water bottle. 'Fancy a sip?' he offered. I couldn't remember when I had last drunk my own water, and sheepishly accepted his gracious offer. Feeling the sweetened hydration swirl in my mouth and roll down my throat gave me a micro boost of energy. My mind clicked up a gear, and the weight of the final few miles of today's ride lifted ever so slightly.

With my mind more aware of my situation, I reached into my front pannier and grabbed a handful of nuts and dried fruit. 'Want some?' I asked my companions through chewing. 'We're just around the corner from home,' one responded, while the other shook his head.

And just as quietly as they had appeared, after the next corner they disappeared, leaving me to cycle the final few miles into Edinburgh more alive and aware than when they first found me. I realised that I needed to be more disciplined in how often I ate and drank if I was to avoid energetically, and quite possibly physically, crashing.

In Edinburgh, my initial plan was to recover for two nights, treating myself to a massage, some great food, and early nights. I accomplished two thirds of this intention, but on my second night, I decided to stay out a little longer than usual. Seeing another solo traveller eating alone, I asked if I could join her and we decided that the best option for my recovery was to reconnect with people and go dancing!

In hindsight, my poor legs wanted nothing less than being shaken around until the wee hours of the morning, but my soul was replenished from being able to speak, laugh, and dance with a group of people. I definitely crave connection and community, and two weeks of barely any human contact had left me miserable.

Singing my way back to my little hotel room, the night was already surrendering to the day and birds were chirping and welcoming the new dawn. And even though I hadn't yet slept, I felt alive and recharged.

Quickly showering the night off my body, I fell into a deep and dreamless three hours of sleep before my alarm alerted me that my paused Climate Cycle was about to begin again.

The longer I was on the road, the more my body and knees creaked and groaned at the constant pressure they were being put under. Setting off from Edinburgh, I had hoped that my body would have reset for the next leg of the cycle, but to no avail. Within a few short miles, the pain in my knees, in particular my right knee, became increasingly acute, feeling as if I was slowly twisting a knitting needle underneath my knee cap. The pain, rising from six to seven and ultimately settling at eight out of ten, only changed when I had to stop at traffic lights, or turn a corner, where the pain would peak at an excruciating ten out of ten.

Slowing my pace, I hoped that I could reduce the intensity of the pain in my knees, but this only proved momentary relief. For five hours, I cycled and squirmed with every corner, barely holding back sharp cries from the pain.

As the sun disappeared behind a cloud, and the first of the day's raindrops fell, so did my tears. How on earth could I keep pushing through this immense physical pain for another two months? Would I be risking long-term injury if I kept ignoring the warning signals my body was alerting me to?

My clothes became soaked as the rain intensified. Noticing some outdoor seating ahead, I took the sight of an open cafe as an omen to take a much needed pause and a mental recalibration of what my next steps needed to be.

I believe that unless we accept every potential outcome, we are destined to attract the outcome we are resisting. My resistance was to stop the cycle. Until the moment, while shivering in the corner of a cafe, hoping that the mug of coffee I was hugging in both hands would somehow heat my entire body, I had unconsciously believed that stopping was not an option. The tour, in my mind, was bigger than me and my health, and stoically I had said on many occasions, 'the show must go on.'

Keep the goal in stone and the journey in sand.

For many years, I had quoted this Chinese proverb, falsely believing that, in this instance, my goal was completing the Climate Cycle. Sipping my now tepid oat latte, I realised that my goal was never to cycle the 3,000 miles around Britain, this was my journey. My goal was to connect and collaborate with communities, sharing with and learning from them the important topic of climate change. My goal was an intrinsic and purpose-led experience that could be achieved regardless if I walked, cycled, or even drove around Britain.

All of a sudden, the tightness and pain that I had been carrying released a bit of its grip. To celebrate, I ordered a second - extra hot - coffee to reflect upon this shift of perspective regarding the Climate Cycle. Until that moment, I had been closed to and resisting the possibility of having to stop. I had collapsed the action of me not cycling the full distance with failure, which could not have been further from the truth. I had been bold enough to give everything up that was constant in my life to embark on this journey. No home, no relationship, no stable job, no regular income, I dared embark on something that most people would have feared.

I was also committing to visit different groups of people and projects opposed my own beliefs and choices. I knew that I would witness animals, insects, and fish being bred and slaughtered for food, and I had already met people who saw climate change as a good thing and the closing of coal mines as a lost 'golden era' for our country. I had also put myself at the mercy of strangers rejecting my request for help in sheltering and supporting me along the route.

Typically, most people would avoid engaging with strangers, yet I was actively seeking out these discomforts, challenging myself to remain open-minded and curious about what I could learn from them, seeking ways I could possibly upgrade or alter my own beliefs to be more sustainable and beneficial for myself and others.

Even if I stopped the cycle on this very day, at mile 750, it could never be called a failure. I had boldly stepped into the unknown, and this deserved celebrating.

Curiously, as soon as I gave myself the permission to stop, the pain in my knees lessened to a manageable four out of ten throb and I felt that I could continue. The mental resistance I was holding onto had manifested as physical tension. Once the mental resistance had lessened, so too could my body let go of what it was holding onto.

Two months to go and I was resolved to keep rolling, with my revised goal shifting from the mileage and focusing on connecting and collaborating.

The heavens have opened

With a revised resolve to continue, the day I said 'goodbye' to Graham, who had joined me for six days to cycle the North Coast 500 in Scotland, I also said 'hello' to almost a month of intense rainfall.

July is typically not a cold or wet month, but the only predictability of climate change is its unpredictability. Last year, July hit a record 40°C (104°F), yet this year, I had to heat my fingers in my mouth to be able to change gears as I navigated the puddles and hidden potholes.

I had five days of this emotionally gruelling road, filled with heavy traffic and relentless rain, before being able to switch the busy roads for more meandering and quieter lanes. On my second day, after having just squeezed my toes into my wet shoes and resigning myself to another relentless day of cars inadvertently splashing me as they drove past too close and too fast, I heard a 'beep beep'. My jaw locked defensively, ready to defend myself against an angry van driver hurling comments about why I shouldn't be on the road. Yet, I was surprised to see a friendly face wave at me through a misty screen.

'Hey! Want a lift?' It was Don, a guy I met only a few days before in Strathcarron while visiting a salmon farm. The cheerful smile of a new friend and a high five greeted me moments later as I pulled into a lay-by behind Don's van.

'What are you doing here?' I asked, hugging him to me, happy to have human contact on a day where I thought I would be alone yet again.

'I'm dropping off a kayak in Glasgow, then off to Liverpool,' he answered, absently brushing off the muddy raindrops I had left on his outer jacket. 'There's space for your bike in the back, if you want,' he said ,gesturing to the van.

My eyes darted from his warm van to the road climbing up over the imminent hill. Don was driving my exact route, and what would take me days, he'd probably complete in a matter of hours. Could I justify missing out many soaking wet hours of lonely cycling and grab a lift with him?

Wickedly, I thought that I could make up a story about being almost hit and needing to protect myself, but as soon as I thought of this idea, I immediately discounted it for fear that karma would deliver upon my idea and I may actually have a near miss at a later stage.

'Well...?' Don asked, as I realised that I had been contemplating his offer for almost two minutes.

'Thank you, Don, I think it's best that I carry on by bike,' I finally said. Hugging him goodbye, I watched as he found a small gap in the stream of traffic and pulled away.

Even though I knew that I had made the right decision, tears still streamed down my cheeks as his van disappeared around a corner. Every day, I knew I had a choice to continue or to stop. Today wouldn't be the day I choose to stop, however much I wanted it.

For me, the hills represented yet another way of peeling back a layer of past hurt and experiences that still hung heavy over me, weighing me down. The hills forced me to choose whether to keep carrying this weighted emotional baggage or to let it go once and for all.

The first week of July had me cycling down the west coast of Scotland, eventually dropping into England and the Lake District. I shared the 55-mile days of single-lane roads with dozens of caravans, motorcyclists, and lorries, with most vehicles impatiently trying to squeeze past me as the roads twisted and turned up yet another steep hill. Torn between constantly stopping to allow the backlog of traffic to pass and continuing forward in the hope of staying, if only one degree, warmer and dryer, I did my best to remain sympathetic to the other road users, and also keep moving forward towards Laura's home.

Dr Laura Freeman is one of many medical professionals who is a member of Plant-Based Health Professionals. This Community Interest Company is dedicated to providing education and advocacy on plant-based nutrition and lifestyle medicine for prevention and treatment of chronic disease. Laura sees the food we eat, the movements we take, and the habits we follow as part of the solution to preventing and treating illness and disease.

Even though we had never met, Laura had offered me a spare room and a home-cooked meal with her family as I passed through her home city of Glasgow.

My brief one night stay with Laura and her family proved warming for more than just my toes and my tummy. Laura shared her personal experience of being pregnant with her second child and being diagnosed with cancer. Shocked that she, a doctor and someone she considered to be healthy, could have cancer, she methodically began researching treatments that could help her heal while also not impacting the health of her unborn daughter.

The more she read, the more she realised that eating whole foods and plant-based options were an important part of her recovery and future prevention of any other illnesses.

She fully recovered and has two healthy and vibrant children who I adored watching as they made food-faces from their broccoli, apple slices, tomato slivers, and carrot sticks. These children saw food as fun, and enjoyed eating the food as much as playing with it.

Even uplifted with the thought of meeting Laura, the five days between Don's lift offer and finally arriving at her front door were some of the most emotionally challenging days I've ever experienced. Not being able to distract myself with listening to a podcast or music due to it being too wet to use my ear pods, I was consumed with my own thoughts as I slowly made my way up and down the Scottish lowlands. For many hours, I slowly turned my pedals inching my way up a hill until, almost by surprise, I'd glance to my right and see a spectacular view of the valley stretching towards a distant loch. And for every uphill there was a descent, which offered little respite from the continuous cycling. The increase in speed only acted as an accelerator to send a chill through my soaking wet clothes and shoes.

The largest burden I carried by far were my thoughts and the inner conversations swarming in my head. I had been cycling almost constantly for 30 days, and the fatigue was steadily increasing in my legs and body, like a riverbed slowly accumulating debris, making the current slower and more laboured. From my outside appearance nothing was different, yet every day, I was starting with less and less energy, less filters from my concerns and less tolerance when I encountered the smallest of challenges.

My many hours of static cycling in front of a brick wall - eliminating any outside distraction - to prepare me mentally and increase my resilience for whatever might happen didn't appear to be helping me as I struggled with yet another puncture, or the realisation that I had overshot a turning and needed to cycle an additional mile to join the correct road.

The long and lonely days brought forth memories of my past. Experiences that I thought I had worked through and healed from. Yet, as I struggled, voices of my past joined me as vividly as the raindrops beating against my skin.

Memories of my ex fiancé, the person who had promised to protect me, came flooding back. Fearful that he might lose me, and using this fear to justify forcing himself upon me, he had tracked my phone, and constantly called me whenever he was at work, checking where I was and what I was doing. I wanted to complete an Ironman triathlon, yet he convinced me that I was only capable of completing a half Ironman. I wanted to retrain as an accountant, yet he advised that the exams were too hard for me and I was better just being a cleaner and waitress in our guesthouse. I wanted to leave him, but he said that I was 'damaged goods' and I was lucky enough that he put up with me, so best not go.

The fury of what was, and what could have been, pulled through me in waves of intense anger and overwhelming sadness. Why had I believed him so readily and given away my dreams and aspirations so easily?

I cried for the woman I was back then, someone so desperate to fit in that I would step over my own comfort and stay with a man who rarely took 'no' for an answer in many situations.

The ghosts of my past kept rolling in as I slowly climbed and descended the Scottish hills. In a way, these five days and nights on the road were more emotionally cathartic than physically challenging. My body shuddered as I let go of the shame I thought I had released, yet still carried within the cells of my body.

Logically I knew that it wasn't my fault. I believed the men in my life when they said they wanted to be my protectors and providers, yet turned out to be more interested in owning me like a precious vase: Keeping me out of sight and their little secret, preferring to objectify me than support me.

I knew all this, and yet I still blamed myself for not seeing the signs, for not leaving earlier, and for also continually repeating this toxic pattern for many years.

Water is a healing elixir, and as the rainwater mixed with my tears and sweat, I could feel the shards of my past finally lifting and reducing the weight I was carrying. Breathing deeply at one peak before my final descent to Glasgow, I took one final glance backwards and made a conscious decision to leave the pain behind. 'With gratitude for the lessons you've given me, I lovingly let you go' I said, quite impressed with my zen-like response, and wickedly added, 'now fuck off and heal yourselves on your own time you motherfuckers!'

It appears that being spiritually inclined doesn't improve your vocabulary!

Home is where I lay my head

Partly fuelled to avoid paying rent for a property I wouldn't be staying in, and partly fuelled by a desire to wholly commit to the Climate Cycle, I decided to relinquish the room where I had been living in South East London.

It's a raw and rare feeling to not have anywhere to call 'home'. 'Where do you live?' is one of the first few questions people ask when meeting for the first time, and I had no answer.

Typically, I mumbled something about being a travelling nomad, and on rare occasions I answered, 'I'm homeless,' with a wicked glint in my eye. I was curious to observe how the person reacted to someone carrying a title that typically invokes judgement and pre-conditioned beliefs within our society. A middle-class, educated, white woman who, from all appearances, seemed competent and 'normal', did not fit the stereotype they had identified as homeless.

My current situation of being homeless, jobless, and single is a result of my past actions. There is no reason or need to complain or get disheartened about what I have, or don't have. I had past opportunities to buy a house, and I have also owned properties in the past, yet I chose not to. After returning to Britain from my non-wedding experience, I struggled with any level of commitment, for fear of being trapped again in a toxic situation. It took me many years to commit to a twelve-month phone contract rather than a more expensive 'pay as you go' SIM card. The first contract I committed to, I had to cancel because I would wake up in a cold sweat desperately fearful that something might go wrong.

I now have a 24-month contract for my mobile (a huge step for me!), yet the prospect of a mortgage still feels too big to emotionally manage. Renting does make my life harder, particularly if looking for a short-term housing solution, but the only clues in why I am in this situation are fear of legal and contractual commitments. Rational or irrational, I still avoid tying myself to one place for a long period of time. My healing journey might have evolved to embracing a phone contract, but no further just yet.

Aside from my infrequent moments to challenge and, hopefully, unravel limiting perceptions around those of us who don't have a fixed abode, my personal experience of having to constantly seek, request, and subsequently sleep in a different location almost every night took its toll on me physically and emotionally.

There is something called the First Night Effect, where sleep is impacted when sleeping in an unfamiliar setting[22]. During my three months of cycling, I slept in seventy four unique locations over ninety nights. There is little surprise that my tiredness was ever increasing.

To compound matters, even when asleep, my mind couldn't switch off and stayed partly alert, aware of the new surroundings and sounds. I slept in my tent on deserted beaches and in busy Cornish campsites (curiously, I felt more refreshed after sleeping in a busy campsite than alone on the shores of a beach, and I think it's because I felt safer with other people nearby).

---

[22] https://www.sciencedirect.com/science/article/abs/pii/S1389945721005876

I also slept on the floor of people's caravans, behind their sofa in a lounge, in my own self-contained converted barn, and also in numerous spare rooms of varying comfort and size. Sometimes, I had the luxury of complete solitude and silence. Other times, I was awoken by cats and dogs scratching the door to be let in, or licking my face if they devised a way into my room.

From an early age, I struggled to sleep away from my bed, where I used to believe that I could only sleep at one angle: with my head to the east and feet pointing west, ideally diagonally opposite from the door. I recall camping with the Girl Guides. I was sharing a room with eight other teenage girls and our mattresses were placed next to each other in a long row. Each morning, I would awake after a restful slumber to the face of many frustrated friends, because every single night, I would gently rotate my body until I was lying diagonally across three mattresses, with my toes pointing west and head to the east. This might have been a happy coincidence, yet it didn't help me settle in different beds later in my life when I moved out of my childhood home and into university halls of residence.

Even though I have let go of the fixed belief about my perfect sleeping angle, and have enjoyed many restful slumbers in numerous different angles, the unsettling niggle of a new place not being 'right' as I attempt to sleep is still present.

I've learnt to reframe 'home' less as a location (or angle in my case) and more as a state of mind. I've created some anchors that help me lean into the comfort of consistency. Most nights, even to this day, I sleep with a hat on my head. I can't control where I lay my head, but I can control what I put on it.

The possessions I own that I couldn't transport with me on the cycle were scattered between a storage unit and some friends' houses. Being an avid quilter, I have a comfort blanket that I typically wrap myself in on the evenings I struggle to sleep. The blanket was a heavy luxury I couldn't justify bringing with me. Instead, I started collecting little trinkets as I cycled through different locations: a feather, a pebble, a small piece of driftwood, and a penny found on the floor became my talismans to help ground and settle me.

Having a home - rented or owned - is a luxury that many of us rarely question. Yet 309,000 of the English population identify as homeless[23], and this number is rising alongside the cost of living. Rarely do we connect homelessness to the climate crisis, but they are intrinsically linked.

As the cost of living is set to increase with increased rent, electricity and food bills, price will become the dominating factor in our buying decisions. Unfortunately for the environment, cheap clothing, fast food and budget toiletries are typically higher polluters than their higher quality and more expensive counterparts.

Globally, we are seeing an increase in climate refugees, as 100-year floods become more frequent and extreme temperatures force communities to relocate and seek solace in more forgiving lands. These refugees aren't all from foreign countries, some British residents will need to seek permanent relocation from heavily impacted areas of Britain.

The Climate Cycle opened up the benefit of experiencing (albeit briefly) different methods of living that might spark ideas how to better prepare for extreme weather while also reducing our impact. One such place I had been looking forward to visiting was an off-grid commune-style collective called the Llamas Community. Each person within this community had built their own house and lived off their piece of land. Even though many residents were fiercely independent, they supported each other through shared labour and swapping

---

[23] https://england.shelter.org.uk/media/press_release/
at_least_309000_people_homeless_in_england_today

surplus produce. The idea of living completely self-sufficient and disconnected from the sometimes overwhelming and frustrating world appealed to one part of me that just wants to run away and hide from my triggers and the negativity that sometimes feel all-consuming.

I imagined waking up to the sound of birdsong and the bubble of a distant brook, warming my toes beside a log fire while sipping a freshly brewed cup of coffee. Meandering outside, I'd tend to my vegetable allotment and fruit polytunnel. In the evenings, after collecting some chopped wood, I'd roast my fresh vegetables and read a book before drifting off to a luxurious sleep.

My utopian dream had not prepared me for the reality that I encountered. Arriving early in the evening, as the sun slowly started to set behind the nearby rolling Welsh hills, someone from the community generously offered to let me stay in a spare caravan sitting at the bottom of their land. It was set to rain for the next few days and sheep also resided on the hilly land, so I decided a caravan was the better option.

The caravan was basic, with a small log fire in one corner and a dusty double bed I later realised I shared with a dozen or so (very large) house spiders, but it was better than my tent (apart from the spiders), so I gratefully accepted. And, luckily so, because the subsequent two days saw the heavens open and rail fall as if there was a man living in the sky pouring buckets of water over the caravan.

The idyllic concept of staying off-grid meant that I had no electricity and no means to charge my phone or computer. To go to the bathroom, I had to walk to the opposite end of the field, along a muddy path polka dotted with sheep poo, climb over a muddy wall and reach an outhouse that was partly suspended in a tree. I could then use the compost toilet before returning along the same route back to the caravan.

The shower was suspended in a tree branch, and the one time I used it, most of the water that reached me were cold raindrops falling from an overhanging branch.

The internet was a laughable wish, and my phone had no reception. After half a dozen times of absentmindedly picking up my phone before realising that there was nothing to do with it, I realised how dependent I had grown on using my phone as a 'time filler' and distraction to my surroundings, as well as from myself.

I didn't have a book, to save on weight I was carrying, and with the torrential rain preventing me from exploring the neighbouring countryside, I was trapped in my own dream, quickly turning into my personal nightmare.

Yet, there were elements of being here that I admired. Even though most people in the commune lived in isolation, there was still a sense of community spirit seen through support being offered to neighbours needing an extra hand when reattaching their straw roof, or sharing freshwater, allowing everyone to have access, if only through a makeshift hose and tap, to fresh drinking water.

The simple pleasure of slowing down was also a luxury I don't typically experience while living in more 'traditional' houses. If I was cold, I needed to source firewood and patiently nurture the flickering flames until a small fire slowly started to heat my temporary home. The same went if I wanted a hot drink. Slipping on my shoes, I'd meander to the tap, carefully navigating between the sheep who were laying down on my path. Filling up my saucepan, I'd slowly walk back, looking as if I was practising for an egg and spoon race. I needed to be quick enough to get out of the rain and cold, but not so quick that I spilled any water, or worse still, dropped the pan.

Placing the saucepan on the top of the fire, I didn't know when the water would be hot enough to drink and learnt that no matter how many times I checked, the water would take as much time as it needed before my impatience was rewarded with the first hint of small bubbles forming, a sign that the joy of drinking my herbal tea was imminent.

It wasn't just off-grid communities that I stayed with. Just outside Bude, on the west coast of Cornwall, a couple generously offered me a bed in my own self-contained converted barn that overlooked their small holding. As retired teachers, the couple committed themselves to making best use of a floodplain - land unable to be built upon due to the river regularly flooding its banks. Due to the rich nutrients the river water and seaweed delivered, this was ideal land for a small flock of sheep and a few pigs. The bank next to this field was higher, enabling the couple to build a polytunnel and grow a plethora of fruit and vegetables all year round.

Arriving mid afternoon, sitting on a step to their home as I contemplated if I should service my bike, or shower and grab a siesta, the husband walked over from the orchard and said, 'you know, you vegans are worse for the environment than me.'

Quietly surprised that one of our first interactions would be over such a potentially polarising and emotively-driven topic, I took a deep breath, smiled and decided to use this moment as a time for my growth and development.

'You're probably right,' I replied, as light and breezy as I could manage. 'But,' I added, realising that my agreement reassured him that I didn't come with an agenda, 'I don't have the luxury of owning land like you. Perhaps for me and my situation, not eating meat is more sustainable?' I posed the question and waited.

I could sense that he was absorbing my words, and decided to gently push a little bit more because, only being here for one or two nights meant that, at worst, if I accidentally insulted him, I could cycle off and we both could pretend that the altercation had never taken place!

'May I also ask, how many hours a day do you manage your land and livestock?' Nodding to the polytunnel that was larger than a few of the caravans I had slept in during this trip.

'At least 6 to 8 hours a day, depending on the season,' And, after a brief pause, he added 'I do appreciate that many can't afford the luxury of not working.'

Smiling, I was looking forward to more conversations with this gentleman because, even though we had different decisions on what we ate - me exclusively eating plant-based foods sourced sometimes globally, and him exclusively eating food he had grown and killed from his own land - we both were open to exploring each others' viewpoints and perspectives of food and sustainability.

I wasn't exclusively seeking challenging perspectives and viewpoints. Instead, I was actively looking for examples of people living slightly differently from the norm and exploring ways we could possibly integrate those elements into more mainstream ways of living.

One village in Wales applied for a loan, submitted a planning application, and after many years of conversations with local authorities and the national government, they finally had permission to build one wind turbine. This community turbine produces enough energy to subsidise the entire village's energy bills. There's also a surplus of money that has been invested in constructing an eco village hall and an electric bus. The bus enables vulnerable and less mobile residents the opportunity to go shopping and also congregate in the hall for weekly 'tea and talk' gatherings. Local creatives are also able to use the space for workshops and to display their artwork for sale.

Thanks to one wind turbine, this community has been brought closer together and every person living in the area is supported and connected.

Thanks to the success of this seemingly simple project, they wanted to build additional solar panels on the land next to the turbine. Unfortunately, this application was rejected because the power station, which imports oil from Qatar to burn and produce energy for the national grid, is unwilling to release another licence to feed back into the grid. As a result, the community is capped at one turbine.

As I cycled past the village hall's window, I heard the dulled sound of music playing as a music group was taking advantage of the space and warmth of being connected. I mused about the idea of one wind turbine - or solar panels - being built in every community and collectively managed. Would that not only start solving the dependence on fossil fuels in our energy-hungry lives, but also help address the loneliness and mental health concerns that are seemingly on the rise too?

Hypocrite

The Climate Cycle was, for the most part, a tour to champion the do-ers of our island, to highlight the positive results they've grown, nurtured and delivered. I wanted to stay away from generating fear or being perceived as pointing my righteous finger at those not doing enough, or possibly actively working against our attempt of improving the quality of life for us and future generations.

As I have said on many occasions, I am acutely aware of my hypocritical position, especially in the sphere of sustainability. I do my best, but I am far from perfect, and sometimes I actively work against what I know I 'should' be doing. We are complex beings, a skin-bag of emotions all bubbling away with little control of what may pop through and generate a reaction to a benign trigger.

Before embarking on my cycle, at the ripe age of 44, I had gone through yet another break up, and found myself questioning if love was ever something I would wholly experience in my life. When I should be enjoying some level of comfort, I found myself renting a small room on the top floor of a shared house with three other people. As best as my optimistic self tried, I struggled to find many positives in my situation and, ashamedly, I increased the amount I was drinking to help with the situation, or this is what I told myself. I could take on many projects, calls, and plans throughout the day, but at night, as I sat in my box-room alone, listening to music through my headphones to drown out the noisy neighbours, I leaned on an old crutch: alcohol.

I knew that I didn't want to drink, nor was I proud that most evenings I'd consume at least 3 gin and tonics, and so I did what any person motivated by shame would do, I hid the evidence.

Between where I lived and the local supermarket, there were no street bins, and I didn't mind placing one gin and tonic can in the communal bin in my home, but any more, I feared being judged by the other residents. The logical decision was to sit in a park and drink a couple of cans before returning home and then hide the evidence in an already rubbish-covered corner of the park. I despised knowing that I was littering a local area, but I despised that I drank much more, and so my shame for drinking overrode my desire for a clean park.

My rational self justified that I would later come to collect my discarded cans, but unsurprisingly, I always forgot and before I knew it, my rental term was up and I started cycling around Britain.

Humans are complex and simple, in equal measures. We operate as if we're above the laws of nature, forgetting that we are actually animals that are affected by our external environments as much as salmon, spiders, or seagulls. Yet, we have created a world that runs almost in parallel to the wild wonder of forests and flowers that is static, unchanging, and disconnecting.

Our little boxes we call home, sitting on a road filled with other little boxes, each one representing another couple of human beings living together, slowly expanding in numbers and taking over the wilderness. We leave our little home-box to sit in a four-wheeled-box, transporting us to another small box, this one filled with desks and screens where, regardless of the season, we dedicate at least eight hours a day tapping and talking into the small screen-box in front of us.

We crave the two days that break this five-day monotony, allowing us moments to be free and do what we want to do, be it sleep, play, or connect with others. And, if we're really good at being patient in front of the screen-box, we are graced with a limited number of days each year to break away from the monotony and explore further afield.

Who invented this conveyor-belt lifestyle, and how did so many of us buy into and actually believe that this style of living is anything better than existing, treading water until we ... Retire? Fall ill? Die?

But I digress, this book isn't about societal revolt against the status quo, it's a book about a middle aged woman cycling Britain who had far too much time alone to delve into the cracks and crevices of society and our Great British landscape.

I am far from being free from 'The System' as I, too, am dependent upon earning money by selling my time (also can be called my life) at fixed hours of the day throughout the year. I appreciate that I am perceived as 'anti establishment', while also living within said establishment gives me the title of being a hypocrite, which I readily accept.

For aren't we all hypocrites somewhere in our lives?

People who feed hedgehogs in their back garden, but also leave out rat poison just a few metres away to eradicate rodents from their abode. (I wonder if the hedgehogs and rats know which 'meal' is meant for them?)

We complain about poor air pollution and dirtying walls from the fumes, yet drive a diesel car to our local gym every day. We tut at the plastic-wrapped imported apples from Spain, yet refuse to grow apple trees in our garden - offering plastic- and cost-free fruit for locals. We abhor seeing cats and dogs kept in cages, yet eagerly buy discounted bacon, oblivious that the price is so low because the pigs are kept in cages, separated from each other and their kin.

We are all just one example away from proving that we break our own values almost daily. Cold and wet, I bought a cheap jumper from a chain store on a highstreet, rationalising that - just this once - it was more important for me to save money than buy from a brand that isn't linked to child slave labour and polluting waterways with toxic cleaning chemicals.

And there are many examples when we break our values unknowingly. We can't be expected to research every single item we buy, eat, use, or wear. This is the role of the government; to set minimum standards and ensure that they are adhered to.

We can influence governments, to a point, which is why I vote at every election and, occasionally, will sign a petition about a topic or cause, intending that it will be brought to parliament and, hopefully, addressed.

On an individual level, there is a lot more we can all do, yet there does seem to be a layer of inertia, or the mindset of 'I've done enough,' especially in regards to climate change and sustainability.

To deepen the exploration of the topic of motivators, I visited an expert in the field of behavioural change, Professor John Parkinson at Bangor University.

John has been studying and teaching behavioural change and preventative action for thirty years, and even though his research is mostly focused on health and lifestyle behaviour, I assumed that the barriers preventing us taking action around improving our health were shared with the barriers preventing us from engaging with sustainable decisions.

Sipping a cup of coffee in the university cafe, my eyes watched as the raindrops tickled down the stained glass window. John had made time to meet me, even though many of his students were graduating this afternoon.

'Let me get this straight,' stretching to place my coffee on the table sitting between us, 'it's not just about access to resources that is the challenge, it's also personal ownership of the solution.'

'Exactly,' John replied, smiling, realising that I understand the theory.

'People need to feel that they created and are responsible for the actions they take, and this is particularly important when it comes to changing behaviour.'

'Let me give you an example,' John kindly added, probably noticing that I was frowning, trying to think how this applied in real life.

'I recently worked with Eryri National Park (also called Snowdonia) to come up with a solution to stop people littering during their walks. Had my team and I asked people, 'Do you litter?' most people would respond negatively, not wanting to be fined or judged for their behaviour. Also, the people who typically complete surveys about National Parks might not be the demographic we truly wanted to speak to: the rubbish-droppers.'

'We had to devise an innovative way of engaging every walker to objectively discover the reasons behind people dropping litter in a National Park, as well as what could be the possible solutions to prevent the litter being dropped in the first place. Having more bins was not an option, as the park did not have enough funds to regularly empty the bins, nor did they wish to spoil an area of natural beauty with big black eyesores on the horizon. We trialled many options, but there was one simple action that out performed every other action.'

'What worked?' I asked, realising that I was quite engrossed in the story.

'Well,' John replied proudly, 'in the car park, we had a small team of volunteers who asked one single question. It was this question that actually elicited a dramatic reduction in litter being dropped, but something else also happened. Throughout the course of the day, after completing their walk, people would actively seek out the volunteers to show how much litter they had collected along the route as well! In short, people we - without being asked to - proactively cleaning the trails of all litter.'

'Wow,' I replied, slightly stunned that one single question could yield such a powerful result. 'But John, you still haven't shared the question you asked.'

Smiling John paused for dramatic effect. 'The question we asked, Kate, was: 'What do you plan to do with your rubbish along your walk?''

I absolutely adore this question because it assumes that the individual has already taken responsibility for the rubbish that they will generate. No judging fingers are pointed and no defensive responses are required. Could I also find a question while engaging with people along the Climate Cycle that would generate a similar result? I hoped so!

Does recycling actually work?

Whenever sustainability is mentioned, the typical response I receive is, 'I do my bit, I recycle.' Even though this is an admiral task, will the mere act of separating our food waste from our paper help reverse climate change?

In isolation, not one act will 'save' us, yet I feel that recycling has become the baseline for 'doing our bit' and not many people venture beyond this line.

Recycling doesn't address the creation of the plastic, paper, or tin in the first instance, so the production of the single-use containers and wrappers is largely unaffected.

Putting to the side that only 9% of plastic received through recycling is actually recycled (note that this is a governmental responsibility to address and improve upon, not ours), when do we start celebrating the added extras we build upon our good recycling habits?

Our individual footprint is broadly made of up of three main areas:

1. The food we eat. Generally speaking, meat has a larger land, water and waste footprint than vegetables;
2. How we travel. Flights and car travel creates more pollution than public transport and cycling, and;
3. What we buy. Regardless if the handbag is ethically sourced, do we really need another one?

Yet addressing these areas in our life seems intrusive and disruptive. Some people might have no other option but to travel long distances for work, so why should they carry the guilt of travelling to earn a living and provide for themselves and their family?

Unfortunately, it's easy to start judging others, and we all have one of 'those' friends who is 'eco-perfect'. They don't fly, don't eat meat or dairy, don't own a car and …. Wait a minute… isn't this me?

Even with all that I'm doing, I wanted to break the illusion that an 'eco-perfect' life exists. In fact, entertaining the thought of a utopian way of living could be more damaging to the cause than making incremental steps forward.

For example, we don't need 5% of the population living with zero plastic, we need 95% of the population living with less plastic.

I decided to show that even I - someone who is seen as living an eco-extreme life - face barriers to being sustainable that are beyond my ability to change.

For the duration of my cycle, I committed to keep all the waste I produced with the exception of food waste. Ideally, I would have disposed of the orange peels and apple cores in a compost, but this rarely happened.

Originally planning to keep all 13 weeks of waste with me for the duration, it became apparent within two days that this would not be possible due to the sheer volume of wrappers, containers, and cups I was accumulating. Reluctantly, I decided to dispose of my waste at the end of every week.

I was shocked at how many bags of trash I was amassing, and people who were following the cycle via social media started sharing ideas on how to reduce my waste for the following week. I bought a reusable coffee cup, some bamboo cutlery and, of course, a refillable water bottle.

Even with these changes, my waste barely reduced, leaving me each week with armfuls of cans, plastic wrappers, crisp packets, cups, and cutlery, despite specifically requesting 'no cutlery.'

It's tough to live a minimal life with zero waste, plastic, carbon, etc. I fear that these impossible targets are setting us up for failure and disappointment, and with a goal that we can never achieve, people will stop striving and eventually and justifiably give up.

I know that I can't continue living as I currently am for many more years. I'm already struggling, especially with the decision to have no car. Even within Britain, a country that boasts great public transport, I am often let down by expensive tickets, delays and cancellations, making a 4-hour trip drag out to more than 6 hours on some occasions.

To generate mass change, I prefer to focus on the 'unnoticed' actions we can all take that will barely be registered on a daily basis. By taking a border stance, we can elicit effective and long-term change through the minimal actions we undertake.

The biggest change we can make is who we bank with. The money we have sitting in our bank account and pensions are being invested in companies, countries, and projects that we might actively oppose.

Until recently, some high street banks were investing in Russia even during the height of the Ukraine war. Other banks still invest in fossil fuel operations and in companies who have offshore facilities employing children for less than minimum wage... and our hard-earned money is funding this.

The saying 'money talks,' is true. One simple switch to a bank that matches our values is barely noticed in our daily lives, but could dramatically help in reducing investments in activities that contribute to the climate crisis. Websites such as bank.green and makemymoneymatter.co.uk show how ethical different bank and pension funds are, offering you transparency to choose where you invest your money.

Another action that I find relatively simple is actually inaction. For those of you who have a garden, leaving areas wild and getting behind initiatives such as No Mow May can dramatically help improve our wildlife numbers. No Mow May invites people to postpone cutting their grass until after May, giving more time for insects and pollinators to take advantage of the early grass growth and increase food sources.

Another area to address is our cleaning products and toiletries. I am always wary of any product that ultimately ends up in a sink or drain that contains 'warning labels'. If it is harmful to me, then it is also harmful for wildlife living in and around our waterways.

Every time I wash my hands, hair, pots and pans, the products I use are being washed into our waterways with the potential of creating a detrimental and long-term impact. Not only do these chemicals put pressure on the water treatment facilities, but with the ever increasing rise of untreated waste water being released into our streams, rivers, and seas, these chemicals are quite literally poisoning the water we, and many other species, depend upon.

I chose to move away from the bleach-based cleaning products for cleaning and also move towards a more natural substance, such as white vinegar, lemon or bicarbonate of soda.

One simple change I made that has benefited both my hair and wastewater from my showers is using a naturally fermented shampoo. Unlike traditional shampoos, An'du has zero side effects on the water's pH and doesn't reduce the lifespan of the insect and aquatic population in rivers downstream of my shower.

Again, we don't have to move a mountain to make changes, focusing on our money- and water-shadow can create ripples that generate far greater results than the initial act itself.

The world is what we eat

I love cooking and eating and know that what we choose to put on our plate has the power to poison or heal us and the planet. During the Climate Cycle, I was keen to engage with ideas, companies, and projects working with food to proactively make a difference.

Unsurprisingly there are links connecting good personal health to a healthy climate, and vice versa. It is estimated that 4 of the 5 leading causes for death are linked to lifestyle choices (what we eat, if we smoke or drink alcohol, and how we move etc.)[24]. When we are sick, we need more support and this puts pressure on our nation's resources, with an estimated 5.4% of the nation's environmental footprint being generated by healthcare facilities[25].

There's also the hidden impact of having more chronically sick people in our population. These individuals require extra support on a daily basis. I believe that our personal health - mental, physical, and emotional - needs to be placed aligned with any climate and nature-based actions we might also be taking.

---

[24] https://pubmed.ncbi.nlm.nih.gov/28523941/
[25] https://healthdeclares.org/the-science/healthcares-environmental-footprint/

Not all food requires the same amount of land or water to be produced. A plant-dominant meal has significantly less demand on our natural resources than a meat-dominant meal. The rolling green fields, that I used to sit for many hours and gaze over, now took on a different perspective.

Henry Dimbleby's National Food Strategy[26] is an eye-opening and riveting read (I'm not joking, it is a page turner). Of one of the many graphics within this report, one stood out to me: The land used by our nation to grow things. Unsurprisingly, the majority of the land used is to produce food, yet what shocked me is that our land is predominantly used for meat and dairy production.

[26] https://www.nationalfoodstrategy.org/

Cycling past the green, green land that I was taught to call home and used to see as beautiful, now filled my heart with a heavy sadness. Rarely did I hear the buzz of a passing bee or see anything other living creatures, apart from a cluster of black and white cows in the distance. With the mono-culture growing practices and increased pesticides and chemical fertilisers, are we witnessing mass sterilisation of what used to be a rich and diverse layering of foliage and an abundance of life in the name of agriculture?

To repeat a statistic from an earlier chapter, Britain has lost over 57% of its biodiversity since the Industrial Revolution, and is ranked in the bottom 10% globally for nature-depleted nations[27].

Our farming practices are killing variety - the intricate web of diversity that our food system so heavily depends upon - at an alarming rate. Farmers are doing their best with the little resources they have, yet government subsidies are set up to lock farmers into diversity-depleting cycles of agriculture, and offer little financial assistance to break this pattern.

I mused, as I cycled through yet another stretch of silent green fields, whether we could retrain farmers to be guardians of the land, rather than producers of meat. Could this help protect our truly natural landscapes, maintain support for the farming communities and possibly help mitigate the imminent food insecurity we face?

How and what we cook can also help us reduce the climate impact load and Dr Hayley Tait, founder of Cooking for the Climate welcomed me with open arms to her kitchen and home.

Every Wednesday, Hayley hosts a cooking class for different community groups. These groups range from school pupils to community workers, and she teaches people how to cook. Using only whole-food and plant-based ingredients, she breaks down the barrier

---

[27] https://www.bbc.co.uk/news/science-environment-58859105

of not knowing how to prepare a curry, or the perceived extra cost of cooking using fresh ingredients. She adds fun and education while also imparting a valuable life skill.

People bond over these classes and, at the end of the meal, everyone sits around a large table, enjoying the fruit (or dhal) of their labour. As an added level of altruism and caring for the wider community, any surplus food - typically there's at least an additional 30-50 portions - she drops off at the local Salvation Army, enabling these mostly overlooked members of our community to enjoy at least one home cooked meal a week.

Hayley's project got me thinking about how I cook food from a different angle. What if each time I cooked, I cooked for two, not my usual one, and donated my extra meal to a struggling neighbour? There would be no extra effort on me to cook the additional meal and, assuming that I'm using whole-foods, the additional cost would be negligible too. Maybe food and 'breaking bread' is a way of us connecting and working together?

Where and when we source our food can also help deepen our awareness and connection to what we eat.

I deviated from hugging the coastline and headed slightly inland, and uphill, into the spectacular Lake District. The winding narrow lanes remind me of a distant childhood and fond memories of running towards a local hedgerow on one of our many family holidays to West Wales. As I walked, I'd scan the rich green foliage for a bright red burst signalling a wild strawberry. Grabbing the berry, instead of eating it, I'd smear it over my lips desperately fighting the desire to lick the red juice off them.

Continuing my scan for things I could use as makeup, I typically smelled the honeysuckle before I saw it and, after a brief inhalation of the toxic sweetness the flower emitted, I'd delicately pull off a few of the pollen-laden stems and dust them onto my closed eyelids. Sometimes, if I was very lucky, I'd notice the more hidden deep blue berry of the wimberry bush and this, too, was pushed around the outside of my eyes, believing that the more I wore, the better it would be. Symmetrical leaves, discarded feathers, and budding blossom branches were carefully woven into my hair at any opportunity along my walks.

'Done!' I'd announce smugly to no one in particular as I twirled a pirouette in the middle of a quiet country lane, feeling and smelling beautiful, though in reality, I probably looked more like I'd fallen into thick bracken and had just recently been retrieved.

Unfortunately, the older and wiser I grew, so too did my haste to see these meandering roads as a frustrating method to slow down my travel, rather than as part of the joy of getting to my destination. My curiosity and connection to these hedgerows dwindled and I started moving east and towards more sensible things, such as sitting in a concrete building and working on very important tasks, such as selling a gadget to a company that already had gadgets, yet ours was slightly superior.

In the Lake District, I had arranged a day of foraging with Wild Forage, a company hosting foraging courses throughout the year and at numerous locations in Britain. I was curious to what we would find in July, a season I don't typically attribute to wild-grown abundance.

Within a few metres walk, our eclectic group of foraging-novices stumbled upon the willow flower, a flowering plant I have walked past and discounted as a weed on numerous occasions. Yet today, my ignorance was lifted when discovering that the young plants taste similar to asparagus! I ashamedly recalled the last time I bought asparagus and pretended to ignore the large 'imported from Peru' label and the even larger air miles that the few green shoots had travelled for my side dish. Now, at least, I had a local - free - and zero air mile alternative growing near to me.

The willow flowers can also be boiled and made into cordial, offering a natural sweetener for any soft (or alcoholic) drink of our choice.

A cluster of wild sorrel sitting under the trunk of a large pine tree exploded into a citric melange of flavour, and a desire within me to eat more. I lingered behind the group to gorge on these clover-shaped leaves before jogging on to catch up with our band of merry women and men.

I was impressed by the range of ages, gender, and also backgrounds present in our group. My assumption was that the majority of people would look like me, middle-aged white women, and unlike me, they would be retired and financially secure, pursuing a passion-project in their recently earned free time.

Yet, our group comprised two twenty-year-old rock band members from Newcastle, a few couples in their early thirties curious about off- or low-grid living, a woman who was seeking inspiration for her art, as well as sisters, couples, and friends who wanted to expand their knowledge and culinary skills past what the supermarkets offered. We all had the same cultural heritage (we were all white and from Britain), yet our backgrounds were pleasantly diverse and we were brought together with a common passion for deepening our connection to the natural world.

Even having discovered more than my mind could contain about the edible world of our hedgerows and wild corners of our local parks, this is a space that is mostly overlooked. Yes, these magnificently rugged lines designed to separate human construction from the natural areas also offer an opportunity for us to blur the lines of how we perceive nature.

Forests, wild meadows, hedgerows, and parks are more than a place to play and admire from afar, they can also offer us a variety of lotions, potions and meals throughout the year. From essential oils, to medicines and staple meals, we are living next door to the largest pantry imaginable.

This year (2024), Spain is facing a water shortage, with some regions already being forced to import drinking water from abroad. Aside from the alarming concern that a European country is facing water insecurity, there is a big question around long-term viability of the food we import from Spain. Will a country struggling to adequately hydrate its nation be able to sustain food levels to meet our needs too?

As we are potentially on the cusp of dwindling food supplies and increased costs, maybe it's time we started exploring the food options growing quite literally under our noses?

Not only can we source food from wild areas, there are also networks of community members turning forgotten land between car parks and train stations into orchards, herb gardens and vegetable plots.

Imagine that every supermarket car park was bordered with a rosemary bush or blossoming dill? Better yet, what if the entrance to the car park boasted a dozen apple trees, or rows of potatoes where, to compliment our weekly shop, we could also pick a few spuds for dinner?

Growing food doesn't require a separate allotment, only available to the time-rich people of our community. Breaking soil, like breaking bread, can bring people together and potentially generate more loyalty and community spirit. It opens up opportunities for connection and exploration of our home-grown culinary wonders.

Seagrown is the UK's first offshore seagrass farm, not only helping support our fish number decline through increasing seagrass bed numbers that act as fish nurseries, but seagrass also acts as a carbon store, holding in up to four times more carbon than a tree! Seagrass is also delicious and with its many varieties - there are over 250 known seagrass species in the UK alone! - it can either be the main course, such as the famous Welsh laverbread, or added to compliment any meal with its unique and tasty flavour.

Lower the cost

For the Climate Cycle, even though the majority of projects were championing positive steps and activities, just like we appreciate a sunny day more after a particularly dreary one, I, too, wanted to bring some balance into what might be perceived as an overly optimistic tour of Britain's climate initiatives.

The more I scratch the surface of sustainability and where responsibility lies, the more I see that the greatest burden of responsibility falls on the group that enables the most amount of pollution: legislation-creators, also known as politicians.

We, as individuals, employees, and even business owners, operate within the rules decided upon by our government. We can only assume that the government has the greater good of our nation and land at the forefront of every policy and decision. We expect that the people representing us are doing so from an informed position, objectively reflecting on the facts laid out by experts, and only implementing laws and policies that help, rather than hinder, the nation's majority.

Wishful thinking? It shouldn't be.

If politicians are truly making the best decision for all, including future generations, why is it that over 100 new oil and gas licences have been issued?[28] This investment seems ridiculous, especially considering that air pollution directly linked to the burning of these fossil fuels accounts for approximately 5 million deaths every single year[29].

Thirteen thousand deaths every single day are linked to fossil fuel pollution. How can we deem it acceptable to continuously support this industry based on this fact alone?

Our energy needs are escalating. Meanwhile, the sun rises and shines every day, and it's remarkable that one of the UK's largest solar farms was completed in just six weeks[30].

Imagine if we installed solar panels - at the government's expense - on every household in Britain? Not only would our energy bills dramatically reduce, so too would the need to abusively drill and damage natural habitats and threaten our already declining and delicate ocean dwellers' numbers. The improved air quality would also prove an additional side-effect from this transition to green energy.

---

[28] https://www.gov.uk/government/news/hundreds-of-new-north-sea-oil-and-gas-licences-to-boost-british-energy-independence-and-grow-the-economy-31-july-2023
[29] https://www.theguardian.com/environment/2023/nov/29/air-pollution-from-fossil-fuels-kills-5-million-people-a-year
[30] https://www.bbc.co.uk/news/uk-england-nottinghamshire-14231678

Only dead fish flow with the current

Cycling around the idyllic Scottish lochs, I grew curious to know what was the largest polluter of these impressive and important bodies of water. Was it the waste directly generated by us humans (a polite way of saying what we flush down the toilet), or was it the salmon industry that Scotland has become globally recognised for? It's a close call because, even though Scotland hosts a population of 5.4 million people, the waste produced by salmon is equal to 50% of the entire country's population[31].

Over 90% of all Scottish salmon comes from farms. These farms are cylindrical wire cages sitting close to the shores of certain lochs, where one of the larger farms is situated just outside Strathcarron[32].

At 4am, donning a life vest and thermal hat, I was grateful that Scotland's summer nights stayed relatively light as I and four other people silently boarded a boat. Putting the silence down to all our lack of sleep, I pulled my arms and legs together, trying to stay warm as the boat splashed through the small waves of the loch. We were en route to visit one of these farms.

---

[31] https://geographical.co.uk/wildlife/salmon-farm-threat-in-scotland
[32] https://www.rivertailftl.com/2023/11/01/an-overview-of-different-types-of-salmon-from-scotland

Gradually, in the distance, I could see the rhythmic flow of our natural surroundings being broken by the jarring lines of cages and what looked like floating shipping containers.

The boat's engine stopped and, alarmed, I looked around, but was met with a soft 'it's okay, we're getting close to land.' Gently, the boat's speed decreased until it slowly arrived at the edge of one of the cylindrical cages.

Without a sound, one by one, the four people on the boat stood up and tentatively stepped onto the narrow platform surrounding the cage. Last to join them, the group had already dispersed, each with a waterproof camera mounted on a long stick in hand, searching for a gap in the cage.

Not wanting to break the unspoken code of silence, I copied what the others were doing and slowly walked the edge of the cage's perimeter. I didn't need to have a gap in the cage to look inside and see what was being held captive, for hundreds, if not thousands of salmon were swimming in a tight circle around the cage. Mindlessly, these powerful and majestic fish I'd seen on many a David Attenborough documentary jumping out of the water, eyes alive at the strength and force they held within, were circling with what I can only describe as a resigned misery of what their life could have been, yet had been denied from them. Circle after circle the fish swam, as if caught on a hamster wheel with only one possible way of ending the insane misery.

A flurry of splashes broke my saddening thoughts as a fish, desperate to rid itself of lice burrowing their way beneath their scales, broke the silence and the water with a pathetic flap. As I looked over the surface, a flicker of silver caught my eye. Carefully walking closer to the flicker, the horrific realisation that the light creating the sparkle was bouncing off a part eaten, barely alive fish slowly floating to the surface before wildly moving and trying to resist the inevitable untimely but maybe gratefully received death.

Where was the humanity in keeping these majestic creatures captive that Scotland so proudly boasted to the world as a display of its rugged and wild beauty?

Overly tired, I couldn't stop the tears flowing as I realised that the one platform I was standing on was one of many dozen cages all holding thousands more salmon, all living a miserable and unnatural life.

Maybe I was too tired to process what was happening, maybe I was a bit naive at why we were setting sail at such an early hour, but never did I imagine what I was doing was trespassing, yet our visit was cut short with a sharp, 'move it,' from a colleague.

The urgency to embark the boat, and almost desperation at the engine sputtering at the third attempt to start, was tangible. With a fourth pull, our engine started and we moved away from the cage and back towards land.

Ashore, and after a long and restless sleep, I tried to process what I saw. Putting the ethical abuse of keeping wild creatures captive, forcing them to live a life in complete opposition to their natural rhythms to the side, I desperately tried to rationalise what I had witnessed first hand.

Did it make economic sense to keep the salmon in one place? Could the fishing companies justify that by reducing the need for wild fishing, they were able to save more fish lives by reducing wild salmon fishing? Take the life of one to save the lives of many, kind of thing.

Yet, Scottish salmon (and trout) were declared endangered due to their declining numbers, so that logic doesn't compute[33].

---

[33] https://www.thenational.scot/news/24111550.scotlands-marine-coastal-species-critically-endangered/

However I tried to justify what I had witnessed, the data was missing to back up the actions. Having intensive farmed fish produced more pollution and caused more irreversible harm to the natural surroundings, let alone reducing the quality and flavour of the salmon people bought. It made no sense at all why legislation enabled this behaviour to exist apart from one reason: Profit.

Strathcarron is a small town in the almost anonymous area of the midwest Scottish highlands. The majority of the population earn their income from salmon farming, and without the jobs that these industries offered, the small tourist trade passing through wouldn't be able to support many families living there.

Yet was there another alternative? A gentler, kinder, and still lucrative option that still connected the multi-generational guardians of the sea to the waters they loved. Could we not seek a solution that ensured we were offering job security and clean lochs these communities needed and loved for their children and children's children?

Maybe so.

Seaweed farms are growing in popularity partly thanks to pioneers such as Project Seagrass and SeaGrown. We are also becoming more aware that we can obtain many essential amino acids, including omegas and micronutrients, from the forgotten ocean forest of seaweed.

For all my life, I have regularly taken supplements to boost my health and help top up on micro-nutrients that my daily food sometimes doesn't meet. Seaweed is a complete source of omega fatty acids and, rather than supplement companies contributing to the ever depleting fish numbers, maybe communities such as Strathcarron could pivot and start building fish nurseries - seaweed banks - where fish could be supported in naturally growing their numbers while also offering a means to earn a living and still stay connected to the water they love?

As a Welsh woman from a mining town, I appreciate the distress communities experience when their generational activity is abruptly ripped away from them. Even though the last Welsh mine closed in 2008, there are still ripples of trauma through lost identity and elevated unemployment rates in ex-mining towns. This experience has me believing that any change in industry needs to support the communities most impacted as well as the natural world we're hoping to restore.

We do need to do better, and do better for all and by all, and I wholly believe that institutions like our government need to step up and be the shining beacon of what great foresight and leadership could be.

Or maybe we need to look closer to home and empower our neighbours to make the change with us that we desire to see.

I know that change won't happen if we consistently lean on, 'we've always done it this way, so why change,' philosophy. Change is inevitable, and we can either be reactors to what will eventually arrive, or we can step up and be the creators of this new path and new world.

Community spirit

From Hollywood movies to local libraries, we are bursting at the seams with heartwarming tales of heroism, where individuals face challenges like the shattering loss of a loved one, impulsively quitting a toxic job, or being bitten by a radioactive spider. In these narratives, the protagonist is presented with two options: either ignore the preceding event and strive to return to some resemblance of normality, or venture onto an unknown path to carve out a new reality, potentially risking further losses along the way.

Of course, our hero chooses the latter option (otherwise, the book or movie wouldn't exist). The hero tentatively pushes boundaries, encountering challenges along the way that serve as reminders of the safety of the old way of living. They face doubts and criticism, being told that continuing on this 'ridiculous path' won't lead to anything good.

At their lowest point, just as the hero is about to give up and surrender to the inevitability of failure, they encounter someone. This individual might be a wise elder like Grand Master Oogway in Kung Fu Panda or Morpheus in The Matrix. Renewed with resolve, the hero presses on. However, even with unwavering commitment, all is not rainbows and butterflies. There are many more challenges to face and lessons to learn before reaching the gates of a brighter life.

Personally, the biggest lesson for many of these fantasy heroes is applicable to ordinary heroes, such as you and me: We cannot do it alone.

Whether we are raising children, embarking on a new job, considering a healthier lifestyle, or wishing to be more sustainable, it is always better when people are with us along the way.

I learnt the hard way how lonely and tough it is when living an independent and isolating life. The year after winning my age-group in a triathlon world championship, I was finally free. Having finally sold my business and properties in Australia, I paid off any remaining debts, including my ex-fiancé, and made the decision to return to Britain. Arriving in Wales just as summer was ending, I turned to running to keep my morale high as I tentatively explored the weighty questions of what I wanted to do, where I wanted to live and with whom I wanted to be with.

Over many weeks, my only company was the sound of my feet pounding against the concrete suburban roads of my childhood town, and my laboured breath as I struggled with the new experience of being cold and wet for almost every run.

Struggling with finding elements of positivity and colour within my drab and miserable days, I attended a yoga class. Anonymously, I groaned and struggled with poses alien to me from the back of the class, and one such pose, pushing too hard to touch my toes while arching my back and reaching above my head, I felt a jolt of acute pain as my right leg whipped out from beneath me.

I later discovered that I had torn a ligament in my hip which caused me immense pain when I ran or even walked and the dull throb also remained with me while sitting and lying in bed.

My only crutch supporting me through this harsh transition had been ripped away from me and I fell far and fast. For weeks, I barely left my bedroom, let alone the house, even struggling with the simple task of making my bed.

After another appointment with my GP, empathising how lost and isolated I was feeling, where meditating left me in tears of frustration and sadness because I was unable to even complete this simple task of sitting in contemplative silence, she prescribed me counselling.

The NHS is a wonderful system, yet it isn't known for its speed for non-urgent care, and as the days dragged by, I realised that I couldn't surrender all control to our free health care system to support and help me.

By venturing to the doctors, my confidence had grown where I felt competent to visit a local coffee shop and sit in a corner as far away from the noise of the till and other customers as possible. Blending into the background as much as possible, my anxiety of seeing someone that might know me and have to answer even the seemingly simplest question of 'how are you?' caused my chest to tighten and eyes moisten with tears.

Yet, gradually and over time, my confidence grew to being able to sit and even interact with light conversation about the weather with neighbouring coffee drinkers.

With hindsight, when I lost access to sport I also lost my identity of being a triathlete and, having moved away from my friend circle, I inadvertently had also cut myself off from a community that could have supported me from falling so far and so deep into the dark crevices of my mind.

Since realising that my struggle was magnified from me having no social network, I committed to slowly and intentionally grow my circle of friends and create a supportive tribe for others to be a part of and not feel so alone.

Community doesn't just offer support when we are struggling. If it's a healthy and wholesome community, it is also a space for exploration, creativity and dreaming.

The Climate Cycle wasn't me visiting, in isolation, small pockets of activity. I was weaving together a web of collectives and people who aspired for a different way of living. They dared to dream of a brighter future and were bold enough to take the first step towards building it.

Imagine if your street offered group childcare to support working parents? Setting up a rotation, each parent would be responsible for collecting the children only once and, working as a group, the cost of hiring a nanny for the final few hours of the working day could be shared between families, rather than paying separately.

Imagine if the untidy and abandoned grass on the corner of your street had wildflower seeds sprinkled over it, offering a sanctuary for our buzzing bees and insects, but also a source of beauty in the summer months?

Imagine if, working together, you were awarded a grant to install solar panels on the roofs of every house in your street? Collectively, your bills would reduce and the initial cost could also be less due to bulk buying the panels.

Imagine if there was a community centre that collected unused toys and bikes and ran workshops teaching adults and children how to repair them?

Imagine if, from the same community centre, classes were offered for children to learn how to grow fruit and vegetables, and each month the children organised a market stall selling their produce as well as the repaired bikes and toys?

These dreams might seem far-fetched, but it is attainable and has been realised by many groups, one of which is in the Cardiff suburb of Splott. The Railway Gardens was a heavily polluted and abandoned site where fly tipping was a regular occurrence. The dark and deserted space also became a high-crime area and a place most locals tended to avoid. Yet, the potential for what was possible wasn't missed by one local resident, Rebecca Clark. Neighbours who equally shared her frustration about a lack of community space and a space to educate and inspire people around sustainable living, The Green Squirrel CIC was born. Fast forward to today, and the abandoned space is now a hive of activity offering free child care, fruit and vegetable beds, shipping container businesses to support startup companies, bike repair and hire, as well as a safe space to connect and laugh over a cup of tea.

The entire site used mostly reclaimed building materials destined for landfill, and even their website is powered by wind power!

Today, the community has significant input over the classes and courses offered, as well as introducing native foods from their birth countries to the vegetable plot and community meals prepared together. The idea of one has grown into a child of the community which is nurtured, cared for, and supported by many.

Imagine if we stopped saying 'I' and started saying 'we,' how far could our imagination take us?

I had more punctures than flies in my mouth

The cycle route was conveniently split into thirds by both months and also countries. June represented me mostly cycling through the rugged landscape of Scotland. July was filled with childhood memories of undulating walks along the Welsh coastline, and the final month, August, was the homeward-bound cycle, leaving the more wilderness areas for increasingly urbanised environments. Hamlets grew in size to towns and eventually cities, and my mostly calm cycle became progressively frantic with commuters pushing past me towards a red light where I would inevitably catch them up.

During my final month, one mecca had been calling me from the first day I had the vision for the Climate Cycle: The Eden Project.

Nestled on the old site of an abandoned open clay pit, photos of the gaping wound human activity had slashed onto the side of this hill had many assuming it would forever remain an eyesore, a harsh reminder of the damage we humans can cause.

Yet, in the late 1990s visionaries decided to create something that brought together technology, our natural world, and the best of humanity. They believed that if they created something from nothing, and that many had deemed impossible, it would inspire others to believe and create something 'impossible' too.

Fast forward to today and The Eden Project is an internationally recognised icon of what's possible when you believe in magic (and, of course, immensely hard work).

Two enormous bulbous domes peek over a green canopy of trees, shrubs, and flowerbeds. With a clear hexagonal grid-like structure stretching over the cylinders, these biomes look more out of a movie set in space than the gentle rolling hills of Cornwall. Yet each year, millions of tourists flock to the site, exploring interactive displays, walking through edible gardens, and trying to count all the species of insects swarming over the pollinating plants polka dotted around the site.

I had visited The Eden Project over 20 years ago, within the first year of its opening, and I recall sitting on the floor of one of the mostly earth-covered domes while helping a group of children bend willow branches into stars.

Today, the two biomes are unrecognisable from that memory, but for the hexagonal bubble sitting around us. The first biome I walked through is acclimated to the tropical rainforest. From the second I walked off the bridge, pushing open the doors to the biodome, I was hit with the delicious memory of warm, humid days spent in Central America. Bananas hung off nearby trees and the sound of a rainforest splashing the rocks and creating a mist around the hanging orchards was music to my ears.

Throughout the canopy walk, snippets of information on why the rainforest is important to us and how we benefit from it within our daily lives is interwoven with the tropical smells of foreign flowers and alluring sounds of the recordings of, if my memory serves me well, brightly coloured chattering parrots. From cacao, to coffee and saffron, to sugar, I was surrounded with over 1,000 varieties of plants that ranged from the 'very familiar' to the 'never heard of'.

Having sent a vast number of emails, bordering on the obsessive, to The Eden Project, I was offered access to the site prior to the venue officially opening to the masses. Yet, this serene visit of the site was gradually taken over by an increasing volume of people and noise. The sheer amount of people both shocked and excited me. I begrudged having to wait 90 minutes to order food from a canteen even with Michael Pollan's heartening quote of, 'Eat food. Not too much. Mostly plants,' painted proudly on many nearby walls.

Yet the flip side of my impatience of getting fed was that thousands of people were so curious about this diversity-haven they drove for many hours to explore the wonders of our natural world. I became hopeful that, aside from being awed by the 100-year old olive and fig trees in the Mediterranean biome, the visitors would realise that some elements of The Eden Project's outdoor gardens could easily be replicated in their homes too.

To arrive at The Eden Project, I had cycled over 2,800 miles (7,251 km), climbing in excess of 151,100 feet (46,055 m) over 70 days. For the initial days, the excitement of finally leaving London and embarking on this adventure, filled me with exhilaration and also a little trepidation. I was cycling away from my comfort zone and into the wild unknown. Maybe, partly I was so in awe of starting the cycle and partly relieved that the first few days of finding accommodation, visiting projects, and also connecting with cyclists and communities followed the plan to the minute, I didn't have time to process and absorb what I was seeing.

At the start of the second week, I deviated a little from the pre-planned route. Preferring to cycle on roads, I typically avoided trail paths for concern that, with the additional 30 kg of kit I was carrying, my bicycle tyres were more susceptible to punctures.

Yet, as I left Scarborough and headed north, I saw a sign for a bicycle route that appeared to sit closer to the coast and might open up better views than a tarmac road.

Initially, the path was very tame, mostly made up of compounded smooth pebbles, yet as the path meandered upwards through a forest, I became slightly concerned because I was already having to twist and wind around protruding tree roots and a few large boulders. Resigned to my decision, I pushed onwards until, just as I passed through a gap in the trees, I was greeted with a spectacular view of the North Yorkshire coastline. The view of the deep blue ocean gently breaking onto yellow sandy bays far below was an ideal place to pause for lunch. Sitting next to my bike on a piece of grass, I listened. I could hear the faraway droning sound of the road compete with the gentle splash of the waves below me, and nothing else.

Relieved to have found such a quiet and serene place to stop, I closed my eyes. Slowly, however, the silence started to become deafening. I was sitting next to a forest and fields in mid-June during summer. Where were the birds and insects?

This memory returned to me as I walked along another Eden Project pathway because the contrast was extreme. Even in relatively unmanaged areas of this Project, there were still signs and sounds of life.

It was hard to leave the serene space, but the life of a nomad only has one constant friend, and that friend is change.

Cycling east, I started to pass through more residential areas where homeowners would busily be dragging bulky lawnmowers up and down their already short grass, or snipping an out of place branch before placing the leaves, flower heads, and grass cuttings into a plastic bag, to be disposed of far away from their picture-perfect garden.

Space for insects to eat, sleep and survive was exclusively reserved for places like The Eden Project, not in our back gardens. By our obsession to have uniform and monoculture grass, we are significantly reducing the pollinating grasses and foliage required to sustain insect life. The lawns also hurt our soil health, by not offering a melange of nutrients to give back to the depleting quality of earth under our feet.

Lawns only became popular in the 18th Century, being seen as a status symbol of the aristocracy being wealthy enough to tame and maintain their gardens. There is no ecological or personal benefit, aside from the occasional kick around with a football on some weekends. I personally preferred to go to a local park to play because there were more people to engage with and a bigger space to run around in.

A similar and just as sad 'creation' was the label of a weed. Weeds are plants that grow where you don't want them to. A rose would be deemed a weed if it grew in the middle of a road, and nettles are celebrated by foragers who appreciate this all-year round robust plant. Did you know that nettles are a high source of iron, protein, magnesium and even potassium! Nettles also cook similar to spinach yet, unlike the leafy green we see in most supermarkets, nettles don't need as much water or tending to, plus they are really resilient and grow like, well, weeds! Why aren't we eating more nettles?

To save our way of living, our communities, our country, and our planet, we need to do more than accept diversity, we need to celebrate it. The rigid structure of society has led to many of the innovations we have today, and while many of these are truly useful, yet not all of them are.

We do need to evolve, elevating from our past and learning new styles of connecting with our neighbours and natural surroundings. If we always do what we've always done, we'll only get what we've always had.

If you believe that you deserve more than a 9-5 lifestyle, one sneeze away from illness, or if you know deep in your heart that we - collectively - could be doing more to support people as well as our natural environment, we need to start making a change today.

Is there hope?

On Saturday 2 September 2024 at 3:05pm, for the last time, I stopped my route tracker and lent my bicycle against the same statue of Winston Churchill I had seen only three months prior.

A small group of friends and supporters had joined me, as well as one reporter, keen to capture my emotions after finishing such an epic bike ride.

Smiling from ear to ear, I did my best to be the person I thought I needed to be for this moment. I gushed stories of being infatuated with the thousands of swirling baby lobsters no larger than my little fingernail in the National Lobster Hatchery in Cornwall. I shared the time I laughed so hard over a campfire in Wales, I had to run to the bathroom, only to realise that the toilet was an upcycled washing machine perched on top of a compost bin. I also shared my concerns that, even though there were many small-scale community-led initiatives run by a handful of passionate locals, I struggled to find many large projects making a big dent in the action to mitigate climate change.

'How do you feel, Kate?'

Numb.

'You must be proud of what you accomplished!'

Not really, because I fear that I haven't contributed to changing the narrative much at all.

'So… what's next?'

Curl up in a foetal position in a dark room and sleep for days.

Yet, alas, I barely had a weekend to myself before I was pushed into life and started seeking work, a home, and transport beyond a bike by Monday morning.

(As per the publishing of this book, I am still resisting finding a home and still only travel by public transport or bike.)

Does sustainability even exist? Can we eat sustainable fish whilst fishing at the same time? Or is complete abstinence the only way forward?

I see on my social media feed stories of civil disobedience because members of our community are so concerned about new laws approving oil and gas drilling, or new roads being built rather than investing in better public transport services.

These people are desperate enough to risk punishment for us all to have cleaner air to breathe. Don't we all want this?

I mused, 'what if more people actually cared about something enough to risk going to prison to protect it?' Are we just numb to the stories of oppression and corruption, or do we not know about it?

Twenty people who are disobedient can be arrested and punished, yet if we were 200 or 2,000 people, could we then have a layer of collective protection and possibly influence the direction of our country? And, even knowing this, I still did not join them…

Standing alone, we are vulnerable and weak. Yet moving together we can move mountains. What will it take for us to start speaking up and demanding better from our country's leaders?

Is this an emergency? However we explore our imminent future, be it through energy, water, diversity, food, jobs, security... we're on a steep declining path towards uncertainty.

It's undeniable that the weather is becoming more extreme. Does that merit a climate emergency?

We already are facing exceptionally high energy bills. Is this an energy crisis?

Food costs are going up and crops are failing. Is this an emergency?

Salaries are being capped, jobs being lost, and cost of living is increasing. Does this merit an emergency?

The number of species and wilderness areas that help maintain balance for our ecosystem are declining. Is this a biodiversity crisis?

Water shortages are predicted, with freshwater rivers and oceans being polluted. Is this an imminent emergency?

Whichever way I deconstruct our society, we are on the cusp of undeniable and dramatic change.

I'm tired of arguing whether this is a climate emergency, or not. It's irrelevant. The consequences are vast and far reaching: let's talk about that!

Our actions are producing certain results. These results mean that certain people will not be able to afford the current living standards, exacerbating issues such as the scarcity of adequate housing, food shortages, the energy crisis and increasing levels of disease and illness. Coupled with the dramatic and diminishing number of species - a core element of our ecosystem - we still seem blindly oblivious to the risks. It's crumbling in front of our eyes, yet we continue to stumble blindly towards the cliff edge, where we will experience the crisis firsthand.

I'm all for experiential learning, it's how I've learnt for most of my life, but we cannot afford to wait until the majority of us have 'felt the fall,' which is coming.

I'm typically not one for quoting a tv series, but, 'winter is coming.' It will be dark, and the people we will be fighting against could be our neighbours and, potentially, our government.

This isn't meant to be doom and gloom and fear-mongering, but it is meant to jolt a little bit of energy into you.

If you think that I'm wrong, prove it. Show me the data that says otherwise.

If you think that I'm right, start writing to your MP and making those changes in your routine and habits.

Change isn't easy, it's not designed to be. Growth is meant to hurt, but it's worth it.

Is there an emergency? Yes.

The alert alarm bells have been ringing for a long time in the deafening silence generated by the absence of life in our gardens.

What shade of amber do we need to see to step into action before reaching the red zone? It'll be a hell of a lot harder to learn to fly when we're already in free fall and without our current safety wheels on.

Even carrying the burden of this knowledge with me every single day, I still have hope. Hope, the delicate flickering light that, when we pause to listen, is saying, 'don't give up.' Britain used to be great, and we have a chance to reclaim that title.

There are many wonderful people on our islands who are doing amazing things, we just need more of them.

I don't have the answers, I don't think that there is one solution for this entangled mess, but I think that there are three constants that will help us change the narrative:

Community

Collaboration

Compassion

With gratitude

I always promised that if I ever wrote a book, the first person I would thank would be myself. I am extremely grateful for the many hours I chose to sit in front of my laptop to achieve my life goal of being an author, even when swimming, cycling, walking, or pretty much anything other than writing tempted me. Thank you, me!

There are many people I wish to thank for their input, guidance and support. Without you, the writing experience would have been significantly more challenging, as well as the Climate Cycle.

Without the financial support from Don't Cry Wolf, Beryl, SF Recruitment and Squeaky, Climate Cycle would not have taken place. I wish to extend an extra-special 'ta muchly' to John Brown, founder of DCW, who met me when this cycle was still a crazy idea written on the back of a napkin. Your belief in me fuelled my desire to turn my idea into reality.

Grahame Sharpe, you are a star. From our initial chance meeting at a bike mechanic course, you have slowly grown to love Climate Cycle almost as much as I do. Thank you for picking up the 'important bits' such as bike maintenance and route planning, as well as your company along the Scottish route. I am so grateful to call you my friend.

Kirstie Lilith, your daily messages as well as supporting me navigate my emotional and energetic journey along the Climate Cycle was invaluable. I love you.

Thank you Tao and Riley for your online support.

There are so many projects and people that I met along the way and supported me that I wish to extend my thanks. I've done my best to capture everyone who contributed.

The generosity shown to me through people welcoming me into my home warms my heart. Thank you Margaret & Peter for a delicious lunch, Geraint, Sam & Will, Dr Hayley Tait & Hannah, Dr Laura Freeman and family Roger, Louie & Sadie, Sahrah, Miranda, Merle, Anna, Mim, Sarah, Roger's daughter Nia, James, Ben, Allen & Maggie, Joseph & family, Scott & Louise, Katie, Malcolm, Ben & Katherine, Sarah, Steve & Ralph the cute puppy, Chris & Sasha and Phil from BRIT charity whose grounding words helped maintain traction through the ride. Thank you Caroline - my uni friend who still puts up with my resistance to growing up, Mao being almost as wild as I am and Anna, Finn & Alan - maybe one day we'll build that outhouse together!

Thank you Riddhima, who helped write to every school in England, Scotland and Wales. Of the 30,000+ emails sent, twenty schools replied and sent a beautiful logo for the Climate Cycle. Thank you St Giles Church of England Pontefract, St Mary's Catholic Primary School Brewood, Unicorn Primary, Ranskill Primary school, Leamington Primary Academy, Gorse Ride Juniors, Jedburgh Grammar Campus, Race Leys Junior School, Emmer Green Primary School, Haberdashers' School for Girls, The Ferrars Academy, Thomas Gainsborough School, Hope Valley College, Howell's School Llandaff, Barham CE Primary, Westhill Primary School, Corsham Primary School, St Edmund Campion, St Thomas' CE Primary Academy and a special thank you to Craigdhu Primary School, who I am now one of the Eco-Ambassadors.

Thank you Kate Dunbar for the spectacular graphics to promote the school project.

Thank you every single project, council, company, university and project that shared the good work that you're doing. Below is a list of projects, experts and change-makers I had the pleasure of meeting:

Rachel Cubitt for organising an extensive experience including New U Enterprises, the Master Composters of Norwich and Gressen Hall, Dr Shireen Kasaam from Plant-Based Health Professionals, Alex representing Keep Wales Tidy, Cirhan, Helene & Haydon from National Grid, Dr Prashant Kumar & Ana Paula Mendes Emygdio from GCARE at University of Surrey, Dr Numair Masud from Cardiff University, Dr John Parkinson from Bangor University, Outfit Morray, Jamie & Don, Carolyn Goodwin, Jane Tredgett founder of SCRAP Factory Farming, Alex founder of Mocean Fitness, Seagrown, The Green Runners, especially Darren & David for your company and hospitality, Westhill Primary school, Aberdeen, Steve Truluck, David for your epic UPSO bags and generous hospitality, Holiferm and An-du founders Tina & Lizzy for your friendship, Eco Schools Ysgol Bryn Deva & Ysgol Felinfach. Lizzie from Incredible Edible, Porthmadog, Sustrans and Cycling UK, Dr Hannah Kerr from The Bug Farm, Cwm Arian Renewable Energy, Centre for Alternative Technology, Project Seagrass, Railway Gardens in Splott, Paula and the team at Forest Green Rovers, Giovanna from Naturbeads, The National Lobster Hatchery, Dick Pearce, The Bosavern Community, Holly and her passion for gleaning, The Eden Project, Ryan from BAM Clothing, Fay from Plymouth Council, Laura Baldwin from Transition Portland, Etienne Stott co-founder of Champions for Earth, Lew and the team at EcoAthletes, Liu for arranging a great tour of Folkestone including a cycle with the mayor, Leah's spectacular fashion activism from A:Dress, the Lammas community and Luna's vegan cafe and the wonderful WVW community.

Thank you Joel, Kirstie and Maria for proofreading the book and many suggestions in how to make this book a better read.

Thank you to my friends and parents. I love you for who you are in the world.

Finally, I want to thank you for reading my book, Climate Cycle. I appreciate you committing time to reflect on my musings about the climate, adventure and the meaning of my life. You are someone special.

If we do things alone, it's a journey, but when we work together, it becomes a movement.

Resources

As you can imagine, the climate world is changing at a rapid pace and whatever respires I share with you run the risk of being outdated post publishing. Resources are also location-specific, where groups based in South Wales might not be relevant if you live in the west of England.

Below are some suggestions of how to get involved in the themes mentioned through this book:

Sustainability
UN 17 Sustainability Development Goals: https://sdgs.un.org/goals
Pledgeball: https://pledgeball.org/

Home
> Step away from large chains & support local, independent stores
> Support companies that offer transparency on their environmental & social impact
One percent for the planet: https://www.onepercentfortheplanet.org
Buy one give one: https://b1g1.com/
Choose an ethical bank: https://bank.green/
Ensure your pension is ethical: https://makemymoneymatter.co.uk
Effective altruism: https://highimpactathletes.org/

Food & energy
> For personal & planetary health, step away from processed food & explore whole-foods
> Reduce, or eliminate, dairy & meat consumption

Health Professionals:	https://plantbasedhealthprofessionals.com/
Switch 4 Good:	https://switch4good.org/
Incredible edible:	https://www.incredibleedible.org.uk/
Green energy provider:	https://www.ecotricity.co.uk/

Travel
> Build travel into your holiday time, so the trip becomes as exciting as the destination

Cycling UK:	https://www.cyclinguk.org/
Slow travel:	https://www.slow-travel.uk/

Nature
> If you have a garden, leave a section to 'go wild' to help increase biodiversity

Project Seagrass:	https://www.projectseagrass.org/
No mow May:	https://www.plantlife.org.uk/campaigns/nomowmay/

Kit
> Avoid buying new kit and use what you currently have in your wardrobe
> Instead of buying, consider hiring or borrowing equipment from your local swap shop. or neighbour
> If you do need to buy something new, visit your local charity shop for 'second-life' options
> Explore natural materials, such as mycelium (mushroom), bamboo, pineapple or cork

Bamboo Bicycle Club:	https://bamboobicycleclub.org/
UPSO bags:	https://upsobags.co.uk/

Speak out & take action
> Make your voice count by voting and signing online petitions

Surfers Against Sewerage:	https://www.sas.org.uk/
Trash Free Trails:	https://www.trashfreetrails.org/
City to Sea:	https://www.citytosea.org.uk/

School resources
Eco Schools: https://keepwalestidy.cymru/eco-schools

Sport & sustainability
Champions for Earth   https://championsforearth.com/
EcoAthletes   https://www.ecoathletes.org/
The Green Runners   https://thegreenrunners.com/
Sport Local for Life: https://sport-local.earth

Please visit www.katestrong.global/climatecycle for more information on the individual projects visited during Climate Cycle.

About the author

Kate Strong is a behavioural change expert, leadership and resilience coach, keynote speaker, multiple world record cyclist, age-group World Champion triathlete, ex-aerospace engineer, Reiki Master and adventurer activist. In her sparer time(!) she enjoys barefoot walking in forests, quilting and has recently written a book.

Evolving from competitive sport, Kate now uses athletic platform to connect and mobilise communities around critical issues such as climate change, water access, and social inequality.

Kate is a sought after speaker on topics including resilience, effective leadership and sustainability.

She also offers personal coaching and a monthly group mentorship community. Additionally, she has developed a school sustainability course to equip future generations with the essential skills required to achieve our sustainability targets and develop leadership skills.

For more information about Kate, her coaching, courses, and consulting please visit: www.katestrong.global

I look forward to moving with you soon,

Kx

Printed in Great Britain
by Amazon